NEIGHBORHOOD HEROES

NEIGHBORHOOD HEROES

Life Lessons from Maine's Greatest Generation

Morgan Rielly

Camden, Maine

Published by Down East Books
An imprint of Rowman & Littlefield
4501 Forbes Boulevard, Suite 200, Lanham, Maryland 20706
www.rowman.com

10 Thornbury Road, Plymouth PL6 7PP, United Kingdom

Distributed by National Book Network
Copyright © 2014 by Morgan Rielly

A percentage of the author's royalties is donated to the Travis Mills Project and
the National Veterans Family Center. For more information, see
www.veteransfamilycamp.com.

British Library Cataloguing in Publication Information Available

Library of Congress Cataloging-in-Publication Data

Rielly, Morgan.
Neighborhood heroes : life lessons from Maine's greatest generation / Morgan Rielly.
pages cm
ISBN 978-1-60893-263-4 (pbk. : alk. paper) -- ISBN 978-1-60893-264-1 (electronic)
1. World War, 1939-1945--Veterans--Maine--Biography. 2. World War, 1939-1945--Personal nar-
ratives, American. 3. United States--Armed Forces--Biography. 4. Veterans--Maine--Biography. 5.
Maine--Biography. 6. Conduct of life. I. Title.
D769.85.M2R54 2014
940.54'12730922741--dc23
2014005077

∞™ The paper used in this publication meets the minimum requirements of
American National Standard for Information Sciences Permanence of Paper
for Printed Library Materials, ANSI/NISO Z39.48-1992.

Printed in the United States of America

This book is dedicated to a generation of men and women who left their neighborhoods to go around the world and fight to protect their loved ones and their country. They are truly a group of neighborhood heroes.

CONTENTS

Acknowledgments ix

Introduction xi

1 Bernard Cheney: Have a Positive Attitude 1

2 Fred Collins: Nothing is More Important Than a Good Story and a Good Listener 13

3 Horace "Bud" Fogg: Even Heroes Are Afraid 21

4 Harold Lewis: You Have to Have Hope. 27

5 Jim Born: Do What You Love Where You Love 37

6 Vaun (Dole) Born: Be a Joiner 45

7 Robert Guitard: Travel and Learn About Other Cultures 51

8 Arthur and Bill Currier: Recognize the Value of Other Cultures 57

9 Jean Marc Desjardins: Know the Value of a Good Friend 61

10 Lucien "Lou" Mathieu: Enjoy Life Even When It's Difficult or Painful 69

11 Jim Finley: Use Your Gifts 73

12 Herman Boudreau: Get a Good Education and Help
People   79

13 Winnie (Whalen) Clemons: You Have to Give Before
You Can Receive   85

14 John Lee: Everybody's His Own Boss and Everybody's
a Little Bit Different   91

15 Henry Wozniak: Do the Right Thing at the Right Time   103

16 Phil Curran: Choose Your Friends Carefully   107

17 Loring Hart: Education Provides Opportunities   117

18 George Pacillo: Never Back Down When You Know
You're Right   125

19 Bill Laliberte: Recognize and Preserve History   131

20 Arthur O. Caron: The Most Important Missions Never
End   137

21 Jim Mardin: Even If You Don't Have Much to Lose,
You Still Have Much to Offer   141

22 Joe Bruni: Be a Family Man   151

23 Inez Louise (Varney) Roney: Families Fight for Each
Other   157

24 Fern Gaudreau: Take Time to Think and Reminisce   161

25 Dick Goodie: Share Your Stories   169

ACKNOWLEDGMENTS

I want to first and foremost thank my father and my mother for all of their help and support in this endeavor. They drove me to many of the interviews when I did not have a license, helped transcribe the hundreds of hours of tapes, helped edit and give advice on the manuscripts, supported me through the difficult periods, and so much more. Thank you to my sisters, Shannon and Maura, for their support and love. Thank you to my grandparents, Ed and Jeanne Rielly, for helping to edit my drafts and for giving me advice on how to get a book published.

I want to thank Steve Bromage, the Director of the Maine Historical Society, for giving me guidance at the beginning of this adventure on possible themes for the book, how I might find veterans to interview, and how to organize a project like this. The head of the Westbrook Historical Society, Mike Sanphy, and the staff there have played a major part in helping me find many of the veterans I interviewed and also provided me a place to conduct interviews.

Thanks to all of the people who helped connect me to the veterans I interviewed. There are so many to thank that it would take up another entire book. Without all of them, this book would have been a lot harder to write and would have taken a lot longer to finish.

I want to thank Michael Steere and the team at Down East Publishing and Rowman & Littlefield for publishing my first book. They have made my dream of becoming a published historian come true and have preserved the stories of these amazing men and women. I cannot thank them enough or even put into words how much this means to me and to these veterans and their families.

And, of course, I want to thank the veterans for allowing me to interview them, re-interview them, and periodically pester them with questions. I was the first person many of them shared their stories with. I am humbled and honored for having gotten to know them. Lastly, I want to thank all veterans, past, present, and future.

INTRODUCTION

I have always loved history. It might have been my grandfather's stories of growing up on a farm and going to a one-room schoolhouse that first sparked my interest in history. Or it could have been the World War I American helmet sitting in his den. Or it might have been John Malick, a World War II veteran who lived in my neighborhood before he passed away. When I was five years old, I spotted him walking down my street. What caught my attention was that he had lost half of his arm. My father explained that he had lost his arm during World War II in the Pacific theater, fighting on an island called Guam. That prompted a new flurry of questions, like "What was World War II?"

My grandparents bought me a subscription to *Smithsonian*. I would read the issues immediately and, when done, read them again. The more I read about the past and tried to understand the events, the more questions I asked, and the more I wanted to know. In first grade, I started watching *Liberty Kids*, a PBS show about a group of kids living in Colonial America who worked for Ben Franklin and reported on the American Revolution. If I wasn't already in love with history, that did it for me. I remember asking my second grade teacher, Mrs. Sullivan, when we would start learning about American history, like the Battle of Bunker Hill or Ethan Allen and the Green Mountain Boys. She chuckled and said not until high school or junior high. That Halloween, I dressed up as an American Continental soldier.

That only pushed me to learn about history on my own time, which I still do today. This has led me to read and learn about the Napoleonic Wars, World War I, the Ottomans, European royalty, the German Exodus, and many other topics.

By third grade, I was already telling people that I wanted to be an historian, but I didn't really know what that meant. On a rainy day, the summer before my eighth grade, I learned what it meant to be an historian when I saw the HBO miniseries *Band of Brothers*, based on Stephen Ambrose's book. I didn't leave our couch until I had watched the entire series, amazed by the courage of the soldiers who risked everything in order to defend America and save the world from Hitler, but also amazed by Mr. Ambrose's ability to tell a story about a time, place and people in a way that captivated me, as it did so many others.

Even after the miniseries ended, I could not stop thinking about World War II. I started reading anything about the war that I could get my hands on, particularly Stephen Ambrose's books, because he did an amazing job at intertwining research with the experiences of average American soldiers. The spring of my eighth grade year, I had the chance to take an online high school course on the War in the Pacific. One of our assignments was to interview a World War II veteran. I felt like Stephen Ambrose, or Rick Atkinson, or Antony Beevor, or any of the other World War II historians I had read, as I interviewed Dr. Loring Hart, a World War II veteran, family friend and former president of St.

Joseph's College in Standish, Maine, where my grandfather is a professor.

As part of the assignment, I read an old African Proverb: "When an old man dies, a library burns to the ground." I began thinking of all the "libraries" living in my hometown with all their knowledge of the past century and how, soon, those libraries could be lost forever, like so many before.

I wasn't sure how, but I wanted to save as many of the libraries as possible, starting with those who served in World War II. The fall of my freshman year, I interviewed Horace "Bud" Fogg, who fought in Normandy and lost a foot to frostbite at the Battle of the Bulge. That winter, I read *Voices of War,* a collection of personal stories done by the Library of Congress' Veterans History Project.

I knew what I had to do. I would interview as many World War II veterans as I could and collect their stories into a book; this book. It would be my first step toward becoming an historian and toward saving as many libraries as I could. But first, I had to find them. From the spring of my freshman year through the summer before my junior year, I pestered family friends, called veterans' homes, historical societies and legion halls, and poured over newspaper articles, looking for World War II veterans. I even called James Megellas, author of *All the Way to Berlin,* about a Maine paratrooper from the 82nd Airborne he mentioned in his book. That paratrooper, Bernard Cheney, surprised me by calling me at school one day. I later interviewed him in his home in Machias.

As I interviewed the veterans, I made sure to follow Stephen Ambrose's advice: "Always let the men speak for themselves." That is probably the best advice anyone needs for documenting history; just let those who witnessed it speak about it. Many of these men and women had never shared their stories before. Imagine all of those burned down libraries, full of information, gone forever. Sadly, several veterans that I interviewed have since passed away.

All of these veterans taught me something; not just about how to fight a war, but about how to live a life. They were never preachy; never full of themselves. Each of them knew that they had participated in something great and special, but none of them thought that they, themselves, were great or special. There was Fred Collins, the sixteen-year-old Marine who used his Boy Scout training to clip a wounded soldier's chest together using safety pins from machine gun bandoliers while under withering fire on Iwo Jima. Or Inez Louise Roney, who served as a gunnery instructor for the Marines, hoping she could end the war sooner and bring her brother home. Or Harold Lewis, who held onto hope despite being shot down out of the sky, nearly free-falling to his death, and spending four months behind enemy lines in Italy. Or Jean Marc Desjardins, whose near-death experiences defusing German bombs with his buddy, nicknamed Puddinghead, taught me the value of a good friend.

Or Bernard Cheney, who, despite having seen the worst of war in North Africa, Italy and Europe, and despite having lost his wife and daughter, emphasized the importance of maintaining a positive attitude. "So, I enjoy every day," he said. "I can't wait to get up in the morning and can't wait to get in the bed. . . . So, I think that is what makes you live longer and stay healthy."

And, like most of the veterans I interviewed, Bernard Cheney was certain that the best was yet to come. "I see you young people and, you know, people say, oh, isn't this a hell of a world to bring kids in," he said. "I feel just the opposite. Just think of all the exciting things that is going to happen to them through their lifetime, especially if they live a long time anyway. You know, you think, boy, I hope they have as much interesting things happen as I did."

This book is certainly not a comprehensive history of Maine World War II veterans. It's my small effort, done between classes and soccer games and extracurriculars, to save some libraries and to share the life lessons I've learned from some of Maine's greatest generation. I hope to save more libraries and I encourage everyone to listen to the stories of their own families, so that they can be saved and passed down.

History is all around us, from the election of the first African-American president to the Arab Spring. The more we know and understand the past, the more we understand the present and how to deal with current problems, which allows us to look ahead and prepare for the future.

I cherish what I have learned from these brave men and women. I hope you do too.

–Morgan Rielly
Westbrook, Maine

Any veteran wishing to record their wartime memories can contact the National Court Reporters Association or the Library of Congress about the Veterans History Project and the Oral Histories Program. For more information, see www.ncra.org or www. loc.gov/vets.

I

BERNARD CHENEY
Have a Positive Attitude

Despite seeing the worst of war in North Africa, Italy, and Europe and despite later losing his wife and daughter, Bernard Cheney always believed that maintaining a positive attitude was the most important thing in life.

Bernard was born on May 4, 1923, in Lubec, Maine, the easternmost point in the United States, where he grew up with four brothers and one sister. The small town values of hard work and a cheerful, positive attitude that he learned as a child would define his life.

After graduating from Lubec High School, Bernard trained with the 7th Armored Division in the Mojave Desert, learning how to deploy barrage balloons. Barrage balloons floated 5,000 to 10,000 feet in the air and had explosives attached to them. When a plane flew under the balloons, snapping the wires tethered to them, the explosives would destroy the enemy plane. Photos of the D-Day invasion of Normandy show barrage balloons tethered to many of the ships.

Bernard later volunteered for the paratroopers because "I wanted to get overseas and enjoy the war, like everybody else my age." Paratroopers also received an extra fifty dollars a month more than the average infantryman, which Bernard mailed home to help his mother. Bernard's four other brothers had also enlisted in the military and their mother wrote to each boy often and saved every letter they sent home, which he did not discover until she had passed and he found three thirty-gallon trash bags full of letters in her attic.

Boot camp for paratroopers was particularly grueling. At Fort Benning in Georgia, where Easy Company from Stephen Ambrose's book and the HBO miniseries, *Band of Brothers*, trained, Bernard's day started at 2 a.m. with pushups in the mud. If he got a speck of mud on his uniform, he had to do another set. During early morning marches, if he got out of step, he would have to dig a six-by-six hole with a spoon and then fill the hole back up after he was done. The trainees also had to run ten miles each morning. All of this was done before eating breakfast.

To graduate from parachute school, Bernard had to make five qualifying jumps. Anyone breaking an ankle or arm on any of the jumps before the fifth one, was kicked out of jump school and sent to an infantry division. Even though he signed up for the paratroopers knowing that he would have to jump out of an airplane, Bernard hated jumping.

"I always said I never jumped," he said. "It was the most difficult thing I ever did in my life, even the mock towers, jumping out of those 45-foot-high towers. It wasn't in my body to do it."

"So, somewhere, I blanked my mind and did it," he said. "I didn't go out the door like a lot of guys and holler 'Geronimo,' you know, and all that stuff. No way. I was probably gritting my teeth and praying, and you finally put yourself in a mode that you don't know what you're doing anyway. And then when you hit the ground, why, you look up. Boy, I guess I must have jumped. I'm here and I've got a chute on, but you don't remember zero. I never did."

After completing jump school, Bernard sailed across the Atlantic Ocean to Oran in what was then the French colony of Algeria. Once in Africa, Bernard Cheney continued training while the Allies pushed the Germans and Italians out of Tunisia. This was the first time he experienced a new culture and living in a land far different from Lubec, Maine, including how locals would "carry the bathroom with them."

"All they do is they have a robe around them and just sit and squat" on the side of the road, he said. "[I]t was kind of handy in a way."

The Allies had driven the Axis powers out of North Africa and were preparing for the invasion of Sicily—code-named Operation Husky. Bernard and his fellow paratroopers moved to Tunisia, where they prepared for the invasion, the first large night landing of Allied airborne troops during the war.

Friendly fire made the invasion even more dangerous for the Airborne troops. Many Allied ships opened fire on the transports carrying the Airborne troops, mistaking them for Axis forces. Bernard recalled the confusion and panic of being fired on by his own forces, and how many paratroopers were lost before they had a chance to reach Sicily.

He landed near Gela, Sicily, where the invasion took place. While fighting in Sicily, Bernard and his fellow paratroopers were "constantly seeking contraband under floors and under beds."

The Sicilians "had more weapons and more ammunition and more food than the army ever had."

Theft was a constant problem. "Anything [the Sicilians] could pick up, disappeared," Bernard said. "You go to sleep at night, why you might wake up and your clothes would be gone if you took your clothes off."

After Sicily, Bernard prepared to invade Italy. He and the 82nd Airborne fought at Salerno, and Bernard was one of the first Allied soldiers to enter Naples. In Naples, Bernard saw how war could devastate a large city. "There were no buildings" because the Allied bombing had destroyed them, "and kids used to pop out of a hole or tunnel down under some rocks."

He had seen hungry people before, in Africa and Sicily, and would see true starvation when he helped liberate concentration camps, but he was stunned at the desperate hunger he found in Naples, and what it made people do. "People—older people that were taking food from children," he said. "You give a child something in Naples . . . before they can go 300 yards, why, some older person takes it away from them."

After Naples, entering Rome on June 4, 1944 (two days before the Allies landed on the coast of Normandy) was like coming home for Bernard, who had studied the city in elementary school. "When I went to grammar school . . . we had a teacher that used to teach ancient history," he said. "She had a room and we had this monster sand table, and everybody, every class, when they got in there, they built the city of Rome, and we built the canals and the bridges and cathedrals and the memorial, the coliseum, and all this stuff. . . . And when I went into Rome and went down the Appian Way, it's just as if I had gone some place I lived all my life. I knew where the bridges were, where the cathedral was, and what was in St. Peter's and where to stand there under the bronze plaque."

Bernard, from a small Maine town, quickly became the paratroopers' tour guide to Rome. Fighting had finished and they were able to enjoy the magnificent city, but did have to be careful because Fascist sympathizers to the ousted regime of Mussolini would shoot wooden bullets, which, if they did not kill the victim, would splinter, creating horrible, painful wounds.

On August 15, 1944, the Allies invaded southern France in what was called Operation Dragoon. Bernard participated in the invasion as part of the 1st Airborne Task Force. After liberating Draguignan and Le Muy in Provence, Bernard was responsible for setting up a POW camp, which is now a museum honoring the Allied soldiers who liberated Le Muy. Every August, the town celebrates its liberation and invites Bernard.

After fighting in southern France and joining the other Allied Armies in northern Europe, Bernard found himself fighting in one of America's most famous battles, The Battle of the Bulge. When Hitler launched his desperate attack through the Ardennes forest, Bernard and the 82nd Airborne were called in to replace the inexperienced American troops guarding that sector, who had been quickly overrun by the Germans. The Nazis pinned their hopes of winning World War II on this offensive and had launched it during one of the coldest winters in Europe in the twentieth century.

In December 1944 and January 1945, "there was anywhere from two to four feet of snow on the ground," Bernard said. "It was snowing and fog, mist, so you couldn't see four feet ahead or back, and about 28 degrees and people freezing and sleeping on the ground." At night, Bernard and his fellow paratroopers tried

to keep warm by "lying on top of each other or chang[ing] positions. Some guy on the bottom, eight or ten guys lay on top of
each other, and every half hour or so you would change positions
trying to keep warm."

Besides the freezing cold, the Americans were also surrounded
by Germans, some of whom had stolen American uniforms and
spoke English, causing tremendous confusion in the American
lines. "The Germans overran our repo depots, replacements
places, and they took our uniforms, and they spoke better English
than we did, especially me coming from Down East," he said.
"The lines are everywhere. We had the enemies surrounded from
within. It didn't make any difference which way you went. You
were running into the enemy. You could hear them talking German. They sounded like they were right there [but] they may be
in the woods 400 yards away. There was a lot of fighting and a lot
of booming and banging . . . but a lot of it was sheer survival,
trying to stay alive, because there were men freezing to death."

Bernard was part of the 551st Parachute Infantry Regiment, or
PIR, which lost over half of its men during the Battle of the
Bulge. "We just were annihilated during the Battle of the Bulge,"
he said. With so many soldiers killed, including their commanding
officer, the 551st's records were also lost. The 551st became
known as the Lost Battalion because there were very few survivors and little information on the regiment. The survivors were
absorbed into regiments of the 82nd Airborne and the regiment
was mostly forgotten until the 1990s when some survivors tried to
document that it had existed. In 2001, the 551st received the
Presidential Unit Citation for its accomplishments during World
War II.

Bernard was injured during the Battle of the Bulge, but cannot recall how. "I don't remember what happened when I went in the hospital and I don't remember how I got to the hospital," he said. "All I remember is waking up in the hospital and having a pillow under my head and sheets on a bed . . . and thought I must be in heaven."

After recuperating, Bernard joined the 504th PIR, which merged into the 1st Allied Airborne Task Force. By this time, the Allies had pushed the Germans back into Germany. Bernard Cheney soon witnessed the horrors of Nazi hatred against the Jews, gypsies, Slavs, and other "undesirables" when he and his new regiment liberated Wobbelin concentration camp in Ludwigslust, in north-central Germany. As Allied forces neared concentration camps, the Nazis shipped thousands of concentration camp victims to a few camps, like Wobbelin, to hide what they had done and to prevent the victims from being saved.

"I was with the sergeant when we blew the padlock off the place and went in and found" the concentration camp survivors, he said. The soldiers found thirty or forty boxcars full of people. "They all were dead, mostly dead, but not all of them.

"[W]e went in and walked in all these buildings, like these old chicken houses, and then as we got there, why we saw some hands sticking out under the sills," he said. "And we went in and found the conditions that were there. They were sleeping three or four, five. Bunks made out of barbed wire and everybody—you know, they were relieving themselves one on top of the other. It was just horrible. And then we found these boxcars full of people, opened them up and they had been there three or four days in the hot sun. They were skeletons to start with, you know, when they were shipped, and no water or nothing. Most of them were dead."

The American soldiers gave the starving prisoners food, but many died of indigestion because they were not used to eating. Seeing what the Nazis had done, Bernard finally understood what he and the other soldiers had been fighting for, and he was ready to fight all over again. "[W]hen you see it, see it, why then you are ready to fight, and of course that was the end of the war," he said.

Dwight Eisenhower, the Supreme Allied Commander, was so disgusted by this use of slave labor that he ordered the local German civilians to go into the camp to see what the Nazis had done in their own backyards. "We went to this little town, and we made every man, woman and child, we made everybody evacuate, and made them march out to this concentration camp, and we made them dig the grave and bury these people that were dead, but we made everybody go out there and walk through, everybody," he said.

After helping to liberate the concentration camp at Ludwigslust, Bernard also helped capture more than 150,000 surrendering German soldiers. "They surrendered to us," he said. "There were about twenty of us. And they [the Germans] were four abreast with all [of] their guns and all the cannons and all the grenades and everything, as far [as] you could see four abreast coming down the road, and we just had them throw their stuff and [we took] the cars away from the officers."

With the war over, Bernard and the 82nd Airborne were assigned to occupation duty of Berlin. When entering the city, he saw "a destroyed mess of blown-up buildings [and] people wandering around through the rubble."

And the American soldiers faced a new threat of violence from their ally, the Soviet Union. "I always felt that my six months in Berlin, I was more subjected to either living or dying than I ever was during the war, because you went out at night and you were always fighting with the Russians," he said.

Bernard and the 504th PIR were stationed right next to the Russians, who were allowed to hold on to their weapons while the Americans had to turn in theirs. The Americans did not like the Russians because of how they treated the German people, raping the women and breaking into German homes, "so we resented the Russians and they resented us." Bernard and his fellow paratroopers "used to go over there [the Russian sector] and raid their supply houses and steal food," he said. "We used to take boats and go across in the middle of the night and have a little invasion party, gunfire and get back. It was cops and robbers, you know, but for real."

Bernard also found it difficult to switch from constant fighting to peace-time mode. "When we were in Berlin as occupation troops . . . we were combat men that had gone into an occupied city, and war was very much on our minds, where we had been and where we had ended up," he said. "And so [the American Military] set up a set of rules. Theoretically, we were soldiers here and then we were supposed to be Boy Scouts over here, all within a timeframe of a few days. I mean, here you've got a bunch [of] combat men that fought, fought, and then you have another bunch of people come in and say 'okay, now you've got to let the Russians do anything they want.' You can't . . . stand back and let someone [the Russians] do it [commit crimes] just because they want to retaliate against the Germans."

With the war over, Bernard decided to return to civilian life. "I couldn't be a peacetime soldier," he said. "I didn't like the regimen."

In December 1945, he returned to Maine and became a state trooper for the state of Maine for ten years. Bernard was the last motorcycle rider for the state troopers and was even Vice President Nixon's chauffeur when he came to Maine. He then worked as an insurance adjuster for the General Adjustment Bureau.

On June 29, 1947, Bernard married Virginia Schoppee from Machias. Virginia was a teacher and principal at the University of Maine at Machias Campus School and later taught in the education department for the University of Maine at Machias. She also served as UMM's vice president of academic affairs. Bernard and Virginia had one daughter, Beverly Cheney Edwards. Virginia passed away in 2009 and Beverly passed away the following year after fighting a long illness.

Bernard recently returned to Europe with his three grandchildren and some fellow veterans of the 82nd Airborne for filming of the movie *Maggie's Story*, about the 82nd Airborne's experiences fighting in Europe during World War II. James "Maggie" Magellas served with Bernard in the 504th regiment of the 82nd Airborne Division and also wrote *All the Way to Berlin*. While in southern France, Bernard showed his grandchildren "pill boxes where I had been shot at and took them up in the mountains on trails that I had gone on patrol." He even took them to a house where he stayed in 1945 that still had the same crooked shutter.

Despite having seen the horrors of Nazi concentration camps, having survived the Battle of the Bulge, and having lost his wife and daughter, Bernard prides himself on always remaining positive.

"I never had a dull day in my life," he said. "That is what I tell people." He prefers to focus on good events, rather than bad. "You remember the things you can laugh about," he said. "I realized that the way I was brought up and the way that I saw life and learned about it as I grew older, why I find that you have to have a positive attitude, and, those things, they happened, they happened, but life—that is what makes life exciting, you know. Have a little adventure here and a little adventure there."

Bernard "enjoy[s] every day. I can't wait to get up in the morning and can't wait to get in the bed." He credits his good health and long life to his positive attitude. "I am an eighty-eight-year-old non-medicated man," he said. "I don't take any medication. I haven't taken my first aspirin. I eat well, sleep well, have a cocktail at night. Never smoked in my life. You know, I think it's positive—having a positive attitude I think is what keeps people healthy."

And while he may be part of the Greatest Generation, he believes the best for America is yet to come. "I see you young people and you know, people say, oh, isn't this a hell of a world to bring kids in," he said. "I feel just the opposite. Just think of all the exciting things that is going to happen to them through their lifetime, especially if they live a long time anyway. You know, you think, boy, I hope they have as much interesting things happen as I did."

Sadly, Bernard Cheney passed away on April 19, 2012.

2

FRED COLLINS

Nothing is More Important Than a Good Story and a Good Listener

"There's a story" for every aspect of Fred Collins' life, starting with his birth. For most of his life, Fred thought he was born in 1926. Years later, some long-lost relatives revealed to him that he was actually born in 1928, which meant that he had enlisted in the Marines when he was sixteen, not eighteen.

Fred had no parents to keep his birth records because he had been orphaned at the age of five. He and his parents were living at the "poor farm" on Saco Street in Westbrook, sharing one bed-bug-ridden bed, when his father died. His mother could not take care of him and so he moved to a foster family's farm in South Windham near Windham High School. His foster family received four dollars a month to house and feed him, and Fred helped around the farm and kept the wood box full.

The mix-up with his birth date happened as he enrolled in school. When he left Westbrook, he had no birth certificate or school records, so they gave him a new birth date and placed him in the first grade, despite the fact he had already completed several years of schooling at the Bridge Street School in Westbrook.

Fred discovered the mistake when he was fifty-eight years old because a relative called him. His mother had been one of fourteen children. That call also helped Fred recall another vivid story from his early childhood, of a family cookout before he'd lost his parents, when he'd been run over by a truck. His family thought him dead and placed him on the parlor room table. A short while later, a cousin spotted him moving and brought his relatives running.

"I had been knocked out or something," he said. "I had come alive again. That's how my life started."

As a young boy with no family and few friends, Fred created new families through Sunday School and the Boy Scouts. Fred joined the Boy Scouts when he was twelve. "That was the only thing that was there then," he said. "You didn't have anything else but Sunday School and Scouts."

Fred had to walk three miles each way to get to the scout meeting in North Gorham at a one-room church, but he loved every minute of it.

"Scouting was the greatest factor in my life," he said.

And the life-saving skills he learned as a Scout would come in very handy, even before he enlisted. At one Sunday School picnic, two girls were caught in the strong currents of the Pleasant River. Fred dove in and saved them. He'd just turned thirteen and had earned his lifesaving/swimming merit badge earlier that year. Twenty-five years later, he met one of the girls, now an adult. She introduced herself, hugged him and thanked him.

In April 1944, as a sophomore at Windham High School and believing himself to be eighteen, Fred decided to enlist. He wanted to finish his sophomore year, though. The Navy and Army refused, wanting him immediately. But, when the Marines said they would wait until July, he signed up.

When it came time to leave, Fred had no car or transportation, so he walked from Windham to Union Station in Portland, spending the night upstairs in the station on a cot before boarding the train the next morning to the Marine Corps Recruiting Depot at Parris Island in South Carolina.

"In those days, [the drill instructors] were quite rude," he recalled. "I'll say rude because their language wasn't something that Mom would want to listen to."

Fred was a skinny boy, barely 135 pounds, but the running and marching was not a problem for him. The heat was, though. "As a Maine boy, I didn't like that heat. 130 degrees wasn't uncommon on the parade fields."

One time, Fred almost passed out on the parade ground. "It was so hot and they stopped us," he said. "We were all standing at attention. I was getting dizzy. I told the guy next to me: 'push up next to me. I don't want to fall down.'" Luckily, they were dismissed and Fred was able to lie down in the shade.

Fred and the other Marines then took a cattle train with bunks to California, before shipping to Hawaii for some final training. The crossing to Hawaii was very rough.

"Even the sailors were sick." Fred had guard duty six floors below deck, but spent most of his time in the bathroom, throwing up.

"Two and a half years, I was seasick," he said. "Every time I got on water." Fred would read books to try to take his mind off being seasick, even reading as his Higgins boat plowed through the high surf toward Iwo Jima. The Higgins boats were flat-bottomed boats used to land soldiers on beaches in World War II. "I would sit in the back, reading a book. Some guys asked me why I was reading before we're about to be killed?" The reading never helped though. He stayed seasick.

Fred was not supposed to land on Iwo Jima. He was supposed to transport ammunition from ship to shore, but his ship landed on the first wave, and he had no choice but to join the fighting. "We all had to move," he said. "I didn't know anybody. I lost contact with all of the guys I trained with. I joined with whoever was on the beach and I moved forward."

Fred was in the front of the Higgins boat when his unit disembarked. Japanese soldiers occupied the high points all around the beach. "They had every beach ranged on their rifles and knew exactly where to put the sights," he said. "They killed a lot of guys laying on the beach. That's why we had to get up and get going. They had no vegetation. We couldn't hide anywhere. . . . They were on high ground and they had you zeroed in. . . . We didn't make much headway, maybe a yard, if you were doing good."

The volcanic ash on the beach was "just like sugar" and made it very difficult to move forward. In the chaos of the beach, caused by the mixed-up landings and the heavy Japanese fire, Fred looked for a squad, joining a machine gun squad despite having never shot a machine gun in his life.

"I was very fortunate," he said. "There was, at one point, two of us left in the squad." The other thirteen had been killed. Fred carried the ammunition and tripod for the lone, remaining machine gunners, crawling back across the beach, under fire, to collect more ammunition.

"On the right, I saw these little puffs. I was in a little valley," he said, referring to the Valley of Death from the Psalms. The puffs were Japanese mortars.

"I remember looking up as we advanced," he said, "and the [American] flag was waving [on Mount Suribachi]. But the war [on Iwo Jima] wasn't over. It had just begun."

Fred's scouting experience would come in handy once again, as he patched up wounded guys on the beach even though he wasn't a corpsman and had no medical kit.

Fred and the machine gunners were advancing across the beach when another Marine joined them. "He was a little guy," Fred said. "I told him to keep down. We're in a fire lane. 'Don't you worry about me,' he said. 'When there's a bullet with my name on it, I'll get it.' Twenty seconds later, there was a big snap in my ear. I looked at him. He had no expression. He's right beside me here. I looked at his rifle. The butt was all splintered. It'd blown up. He's still standing there, so I pulled his jacket open and there was a hole so big that I could watch his lungs trying to get air. You've got to have suction to have your lungs working."

Telling this story, nearly seventy years later, Fred paused before continuing. "You've got to remember," he said. "I'm just sixteen years old. I'm just a kid. But I had been in Scouts and we had first aid merit badges. . . . There were only three of us there. I had to fix this guy somehow."

Fred took the big safety pins off the machine gun bandoliers. "I pulled off a dozen of those and I zippered him right up. And then I hollered for a stretcher." Fred and another soldier carried him to the back lines. As they raced across the beach, the Japanese machine gun fire went right through the other man's legs. "I said 'Don't change your stride. The Japanese have zeroed you in and they're shooting right between your legs." Fred got the injured Marine to the hospital ship, but does not know if he survived.

Fred remained on Iwo Jima throughout the invasion, then shipped to Guam to battle continuing Japanese resistance there, before returning to Hawaii, where he was supposed to train for the invasion of Japan, but the war ended.

After the war, Fred returned to his foster family's farm in Windham, graduated from Windham High School, and began working at the S. D. Warren Paper Mill and painting houses. Fred married his wife, Geneva, in 1949, moving to her family's farm (now the nursing home across from the Westbrook Community Center) to take care of her sick, widowed mother.

Fred had stayed in the Marine Reserves and, in 1950, was called back to active duty as a drill sergeant at Parris Island, training the Marines to fight in the Korean War. He was discharged later that year because he had broken his leg in a motorcycle accident the previous year at home before he was called back up. His ankle never healed, hurting all the time, particularly while he was running with the recruits.

Fred then returned to Westbrook, working at the mill and painting houses, while he and Geneva raised their six children: Steve, Gary, David, Elizabeth, John, and Martha. Fred also reconnected with Scouts through his children, helping the troop in a variety of roles over the years, including as Scoutmaster. Geneva was also a Cub Scout teacher for many years. Fred has been involved with the Boy Scouts for seventy-three years and still carries a membership card.

"Scouting was a great help to me in all of life," he said.

After retiring from the paper mill, Fred painted houses full-time, then converted Geneva's family's Rocky Hill farm into a nursing home in the 1990's.

Fred had always loved stories, but it was at the nursing home that he discovered what it meant to be a good listener, spending hours listening to the residents' stories.

"Old folks," he said. "They're retired. They need you to love them."

Fred even recorded their stories and gave the tapes to their children after a resident would pass away.

"They get home after the funeral and they'd be so happy to hear their mother, telling stories," he said.

Fred also teaches the Scouts about the importance of listening to stories.

"Stories interest kids," he said. "Younger people can listen to older folks if they have an ear."

"Good parents" instruct their kids, Fred continued. "There's nothing like a good story. I love biographies."

Fred spends a lot of time writing essays and poems about his war memories so that younger generations can learn from his experiences.

"The service has made me more aware of the world around me and of the high cost of freedom," he said.

One of Fred's poems, titled "Those Who Stayed," was published in *The Journal of the Iwo Jima Survivors*. It begins:

> *When twilight falls, I hear the call*
> *Of those who fall.*
> *I think of the life they might have lived,*
> *If the snipers bullet would*
> *Have missed.*

With so many World War II veterans now gone, Fred knows that it is more important than ever to tell their stories, and he hopes people are listening.

"The secret to life is listening," he said. "A lot of people don't listen. You don't learn a damn thing by talking. It's listening."

3

HORACE "BUD" FOGG

Even Heroes Are Afraid

Born May 29, 1924, and raised in Gorham, Bud Fogg spent his growing-up years working his grandparents' farm, picking apples, harvesting hay, tending the cows and pigs and even working the blacksmith shop. His great-uncle nicknamed him Bud, but "[d]on't ask me why. He gave me 'Bud' and it's been with me for 88 years."

By the time America entered World War II, Bud was working in the South Portland shipyard as a welder. On March 11, 1943, Bud was drafted into the Army and sent for basic training at Fort Devens, Massachusetts, before being assigned to the 8th Armored Division in North Carolina as a truck driver.

As D-Day approached, though, Bud was selected as a replacement soldier, assigned to the 83rd Infantry Division, and, in May 1944, shipped out on a Liberty ship, made in the same South Portland shipyard where he had worked, to participate in the invasion of Normandy. It took the convoy twelve days to cross the Atlantic Ocean, "and twelve days I was sick," Bud said. "I had a buddy that lived outside of Baltimore who was never around water and never got sick. He would go to the kitchen and get me crackers or an apple."

After training in England, Bud arrived in Normandy almost one month after D-Day (June 6, 1944), joining a unit that was half veterans and half replacement soldiers, like him. Less than a month after D-Day, the beaches at Normandy were packed, busy places, with "thousands and thousands of trucks coming off the beach." And Nazi resistance was still intense, as Bud's unit fought "hedgerow to hedgerow."

Conditions were often chaotic and confusing. One night, as Bud and another soldier slept in a foxhole, his outfit pulled back, but did not wake them. When Bud and the other soldier woke up, there was "not a soul in sight." The two men retreated alone, shortly after midnight, zigzagging to avoid the German soldiers close by, until they ran into an American jeep that took them back to their unit.

As Bud's unit struggled its way through the hedgerows against fierce German resistance, the combat was close, often face-to-face. After Normandy, Bud's unit moved to Orleans, France, to try to capture 20,000 soldiers holed up on an island in the Loire River.

"There were a lot of young women there who had been removed from Paris by their families," he said. Two women from the village brought chicken and homemade bread to his squad. Bud even briefly dated one of the girls, sitting on a hill overlooking the French countryside while her grandmother kept watch.

After convincing the Germans to surrender, Bud's unit experienced first-hand the frigid conditions and desperate fighting during the Battle of the Bulge, beginning in mid-December 1944. In one incident, Bud found himself face to face with a German soldier, unable to fire because his gun was frozen. Bud had just become a squad leader when he came across a German machine gun nest and called in the artillery. Just then, a young German soldier came around the corner. He and Bud faced each other, feet apart, both surprised.

"He pulled his gun up," Bud said. "I pulled mine up. His was frozen. My gun was frozen. We couldn't kill each other then. Each was frozen." Both men retreated and Bud relayed the location of the machine gun nest to his commanding officer. And he realized "from now on, I better make sure [his M-1] is working right."

Tank fights at night were extremely frightening. As the German Tiger Tanks came through the woods, "there we were, we just had guns. I didn't even have my bazooka yet." Bud recalled veteran soldiers shell-shocked, breaking down and crying. Bud had to hide one sobbing soldier in a ravine until the Tiger Tank passed by. "We were all scared," he said.

Bud was even knocked unconscious by artillery shells twice and just missed being hit by a phosphorus shell at St. Vith in Belgium just before the Battle of the Bulge. He was shot in the head with a round of shrapnel, but was treated by a field medic, and kept fighting. Like many soldiers who fought during the Battle of the Bulge in what was one of the coldest winters in memory, Bud suffered severe frostbite on his feet.

After being treated in a hospital in Paris for frostbite, Bud was flown back to the States, landing in Presque Isle, before continuing to North Carolina, where he spent fourteen months recuperating. After the war, he ultimately had six operations to try to fix his foot, but had it amputated because of the lasting and severe damage he had suffered from frostbite.

By the time Bud was discharged on March 15, 1946, he had reached the rank of Staff Sergeant and squad leader and received three Bronze Stars, the Purple Heart, a Good Conduct Medal, the American Campaign Medal, and the Victory Medal. And, he had met Marie Beckwith while on furlough. After going to a wrestling match together, they fell in love, and married on January 22, 1946, two months before he was discharged.

After the war, Bud went to work at a canning factory in Gorham, then made engines for refrigerators, before going to work for S.D. Warren, where he supplied materials to make paper and recycled defective paper for almost thirty-eight years while he and his wife raised their two daughters and three sons. Marie passed away four years ago, at the age of eighty. Bud is now eighty-eight, and enjoys his fourteen grandchildren, twenty-one great-grandchildren, and five great-great-grandchildren. He also enjoys visiting Memorial Post No. 197 at noon every day.

Bud was nineteen years old when he shipped out, turning twenty after arriving in Europe. "I was a greenhorn," he said. "We didn't know nothing."

Facing the tense horror of war at such a young age, Bud admits: "I was afraid." While some soldiers did not seem scared—"they would get hit and they'd keep right on going"—most, like Bud, were afraid. He remembers one soldier who could not stop thinking about his wife and young child back home and left his unit despite Bud's warning that he would spend the rest of his life in prison.

"Worst thing . . . was when I seen my buddies get killed," Bud said. "I'd always say, well, the next bullet's got my name on it, or the next shell's going to get me." It was at those moments that he would think of his family and friends back home. "When I was over there, things went through my mind, you know, thinking back on my father and mother, brothers and sisters, friends, if I'd ever get back to see them.

"At times, I was a little bad off," he said, but he did what he had to do. He tried to take his mind off the danger and never forgot the importance of a sense of humor, of remaining loyal to his family back home, and of what he was fighting for.

His time in the service made him realize "there are some bad people out there." It was his job to fight the enemy.

"We went over there and we knew we had to protect the USA," he said. Even though he was injured and lost a foot to frostbite, he counts himself as "one of the lucky ones."

And he is proud of his service.

"I didn't want to be a hero," he said. But he is.

4

HAROLD LEWIS

You Have to Have Hope.

Born on November 30, 1923, Harold was the youngest of six children raised on Duck Pond Road in the Prides Corner area of Westbrook. On December 7, 1941, when the Japanese attacked Pearl Harbor, Harold and his brother had just come in for lunch after a morning spent cutting logs on his grandfather's lot. His mother told them of the attack.

"Of course, we didn't even know where Pearl Harbor was," he said.

Harold graduated from Westbrook High School in June 1942 and that December he enlisted in the Army Air Force. He shipped out that evening to Fort Devens, Massachusetts, without even the chance to say goodbye to his family. From there, Harold moved to Miami for basic training, then to Buckley Field, Colorado, the following February to learn how to disassemble machine guns and to synchronize them to fire between the propeller blades of P-38's.

Then he was off to air gunnery school in Harlingen, Texas, where he learned how to shoot down planes. He and the other gunnery recruits started by riding in the back of trucks, shooting skeet with 12-gauge shotguns, to learn how to lead a target.

"You have to lead an airplane quite a distance if it is any distance away," he said.

Harold then flew in a two-seater AT6 trainer, shooting a .30 caliber machine gun at a target trailing from another AT6. After graduating from gunnery school and then learning heavy bombardment armament in Utah, Harold finally joined his crew in Boise, Idaho, and started flight training on B-24 Liberators. On December 16, 1943, Harold and his crew flew to Hamilton Field, California, to pick up their new B-24. After stops in Florida, Trinidad, Brazil, Dakar (the capital of Senegal), French Morocco and Tunisia, Harold arrived at his permanent base in Stornara, Italy, where they were assigned to the 456th Bombers Group, 747th Squadron. Stornara is a small farming town in southeast Italy.

Harold was the tail gunner and in charge of armament. His first mission, to bomb German headquarters on the beach at Anzio, was scrubbed because of heavy cloud cover. Their second mission, to bomb the German lines at Anzio, was the stuff of movies.

It was February 17, a "beautiful day," as Harold and his crew flew across Italy and up the coast toward their target. "I remember seeing an active volcano in one of the mountains at that time," he said.

"We were the tail plane on this last mission," Harold recalled. "I hadn't seen an airplane or anything for that entire trip, because of being the tail gunner with all the other planes ahead of us." After they dropped their bombs under heavy fire, Harold spotted one B-24 lagging behind, its number one engine on fire.

"After I looked at the plane that was trailing behind us, I saw three fighters coming up in back of us," he said. "When they got within 1,000 yards, I gave them a short burst. They were coming in three abreast. I was shooting at the middle plane. When they got within about 600 yards, I leveled right on top of a nose and pulled the trigger again. I saw a flash in the middle one and then all the planes pulled away."

Harold looked for the B-24, but it was spiraling down, one wing gone. Just then, another group of fighters attacked, knocking out all power to Harold's gun turret. He could move the machine guns by hand, but could not fire them because the ammunition required an electrically-powered booster to feed it into the gun.

"The next two or three attacks they made on the tail, they were kind of cautious, but after they realized I wasn't shooting at them, of course they got a little braver then," he said. "I could hear them coming in from different directions on the plane." A piece of shrapnel hit Harold in the foot. His radio operator was shot in the chest. His plane was trailing smoke and a piece of the tail began to tear away. As smoke filled the plane, the first engineer ordered Harold to bail out.

Harold's parachute was full of holes, but he snapped it on and jumped.

"When I bailed out, I pulled the rip cord and nothing happened," he said. "I threw the rip cord away. I unsnapped the cord cover so I could see the two pins that hold the chute pack together with about a 16-inch cable pulling through them. The right cable had pulled out but the left cable was cut in two by shrapnel."

Harold had jumped out at 22,000 feet and his parachute would not open.

"It was very quiet after the noise from the plane," he said. "The only noise was the wind rushing by at 125 miles an hour."

Harold had an electric jumpsuit on to keep him warm, but his electric gloves were not working. "My hands were real cold," he said, "because it's 30 degrees below zero up there." Harold had removed his right glove to pull the rip cord, but now, "[n]o matter how I tried, I could not close that hand enough to pull the short piece out of the other side with my right hand. I tried a number of times, but because my hand was so stiff, I could not close it tightly enough to pull the cable out. I looked down and observed the ground rushing up very quickly and everything was a lot larger than when I looked down before, when I had bailed."

Harold knew he was going to die unless he figured out something, but he did not despair. "You have to have hope, you know," he said.

Just before hitting the ground, Harold pulled the glove off his left hand and was able to yank the cable. "The chute opened and I looked up to see many holes in the canopy, but none of the cords were broken," he said. "When it opened, I blacked out for just a second. Then I looked down and I had just time enough to figure out how to land. I blacked out again when I hit the ground."

Harold was behind enemy lines and was injured, although he would not know how severely injured for weeks to come. His hands were so frostbitten that the skin on the fingers on his left hand peeled down to the first joint. The skin on the fingers on his right hand, which had been exposed for the entire fall, peeled down to the middle knuckles. His foot wound, which was minor but would go untreated for months, eventually led to the amputation of his foot in 1950 at the Veteran's Home in Togus, Maine.

Harold had landed amid snow-covered mountains, near a stream and a road. He unhooked his harness and gathered up his parachute, thankful to be alive. "That's when I figured I was going to live through the war," he said.

In fact, he figured that he was alive because his chute had failed to open until the last moment. "No one was coming after me because I didn't pull my chute until the last second, so the Germans didn't have time to track or spot me in the sky."

Nearby, an older man led a cow and three young children. Harold asked him if there were any Germans around. "I couldn't speak any Italian and he couldn't speak any English, but I could tell by the way he was talking that there were plenty of Germans around."

Yet, once again, he refused to give up hope. He gave his parachute to the older man and climbed to the top of the nearest mountain, toward the west. He could hear the "steady constant roar of the artillery at Anzio beach head." As he descended the western side of the mountain, toward the valley below, he caught a break.

He met a young boy with a herd of sheep, who shared his bread and cheese with Harold. Together, they watched the German trucks and troops moving a half mile below. At suppertime, the boy took the sheep and Harold down the mountain to his home. But first, Harold had to cross a road without being spotted. On the first try, he was half-way across when a German motorcycle approached. He quickly jumped behind a stone wall. When he tried again, more traffic came, and he jumped back behind the stone wall. The third time was a charm, and he made it to the boy's home.

The boy's family welcomed him and fed him freshly cooked sheep curds. Then he spent the night in a grass hut where the boy slept, near the sheep. The next morning, after being shown how to suck a raw egg, Harold met a villager who spoke English; a former Italian soldier named Olivetta, who took him back to his house, where Harold spent the next month. Olivetta had worked in the United States and then returned to Italy to gather his family, but war broke out and the Italian dictator, Mussolini, would not let Olivetta or other Italians leave. Instead, he had been forced to fight in the Italian Army, which had surrendered the previous September. Olivetta's home was on the side of a mountain, fifty yards from the road. It had no electricity, plumbing or running water, no telephone and no stove. Harold slept on a couch on the first floor.

When Nazi soldiers would drive past, he would hide inside the house or in the family's orchard. One time, Harold fell asleep on the couch while some Nazi soldiers were outside. "That time, I got up and forgot that they were there," he said. "When I came out, the motorcycle was just off the stairs in front of the house. Here I am at the bottom of the stairs with the motorcycle so close I could touch it. I didn't waste any time getting down into the orchard, because I didn't know where they were."

But Harold escaped capture. After an Italian shot two Germans, Olivetta's nephew, Carlmony, hid Harold in a schoolhouse before moving him back up the mountain. In retaliation for the shooting, the Nazi soldiers rounded up about thirty men, including Olivetta, and forced them to dig trenches. Olivetta later escaped.

Meanwhile, Harold stayed with two stranded British soldiers he had met, moving from grass hut to grass hut, using the silk map Harold had received during training. When the weather warmed, they would sleep in the wheat fields. During the day, Harold and the British soldiers would watch the Germans maneuver. At night, American planes would drop "million candle-power parachute lights," illuminating the countryside. "If you were sleeping outside in a wheat field," he said, "it felt as though they were looking right at you."

However, Harold never strayed far from where he initially landed. "The entire time I was behind German lines, it was all spent within a square mile area," he said.

Harold's hope for survival was rewarded time and time again by the Italians' generosity and willingness to risk themselves to help him. The Germans offered a reward of $50,000 for the capture of airmen, but no Italian turned him in. "I found the Italian people to be very generous," he said. "Any of them would feed you or give you wine."

By the end of May 1944, the Allied forces had pushed the Germans out of the area of Italy where Harold was, so he said goodbye to the families who had sheltered him, and made his way to the British 8th Army base in Anagni with the two British soldiers he had met. He arrived at their base on June 6, after four months of hiding. The British Army gave him a ride to the American Air Force base in Naples, where he tried to send a telegram to his mother, letting her know that he was alive and free, but Army censors would not let him send it. A week later, he finally returned to his old air base on the eastern Italian coast. After giving some speeches to his unit about his time behind enemy lines, Harold was flown back to the United States. Harold also learned that six members of his crew died and three were captured when their plane was shot down. He was the only crew member to survive and escape.

Immediately upon landing in New York, he sent a telegraph to his mother, saying: "I am in New York and in the best of health. I expect to be home in a couple of days, your loving son Harold." What Harold did not know was that the only word his parents had received was a telegram from the Army on March 11, 1944, informing them that Harold was missing in action." Harold's telegram was the first word they received that he was alive and free.

"My mother and father went through a lot because they didn't know, no one knew, what happened to me," he said.

His parents did not receive the Army telegram informing them that he had been found until a month after he returned home.

After a brief furlough, Harold, now a staff sergeant, was transferred to a B-24 air base in Savannah, Georgia, where he helped train crews and repaired machine guns. A year later, in June 1945, Harold got married. The following November, he was discharged and returned to Maine.

"I couldn't wait to get back to Maine," he said. "This state has everything, but more snow."

Like many people of their generation, Harold and his wife quickly put the war behind them, raising nine children while he worked at Humpty Dumpty for thirty-five years. He rarely talked about his war experiences. "My mother and father never asked me a question about me behind the lines," he said. "I never told them anything."

It was not until one of his daughters asked him to write down his experiences that he finally did, in 2003, recalling how, in 1944, he held onto hope despite being shot down out of the sky, nearly free-falling to his death, and spending four months behind enemy lines. And how he survived to live a long and happy life as a result.

5

JIM BORN

Do What You Love Where You Love

For Jim Born, life is about doing what you love where you love.

Jim was born in 1922 in Denver, Colorado, splitting his time between Denver and Fort Collins as his family followed his father, who worked for the railroad. He loved hiking and climbing, but hated fishing, so when his father would fish, Jim would climb the nearby mountains. "My mother would be worried about whether I was going to come down off that mountain or not," he said.

After graduating from high school in 1940, Jim attended Colorado State University in Fort Collins. By the end of his sophomore year, Jim "was getting antsy about the war and doing something about it, so I went to the Navy in Fort Collins and talked with the recruiter about getting into the Navy Air Force and he said 'you'd never get in because you have glasses.'" That only temporarily delayed Jim. That summer, in Denver, "I went down to the Navy recruiting and I said that I'd decided I'd like to join the Navy as a radioman and the chief petty officer started asking me questions and he found out that I had two years of college," so he recommended officers' training. Jim could be in the Navy, but still finish college. "That sounded like a good idea," Jim said, and so he enlisted.

The summer between his junior and senior years, Jim received a notice to report to active duty. The Navy sent him to the University of Colorado in Boulder as an apprentice seaman. That year was filled with engineering courses and early morning drills. Jim's room was in a former girls' dormitory, at the far end of the hall from the Marine who was supposed to be performing bed checks and enforcing curfews. "After hours, the path to get into the dorm was through our window. I don't know how many kids came through our window to get in, even during a snowstorm. The Marines were running the desk and they were pretty good about not seeing every infraction."

Jim graduated in spring 1944 and the Navy sent him to Camp Perry in Virginia for midshipmen school. Sixty days later, Jim was a midshipman and a member of the Civil Engineering Corps. The Navy then sent him to officers' training in Rhode Island. The newly-minted ensign then caught a train to San Francisco.

"The trains during that period of time were something to behold," he said. "Trains were packed. The equipment was not in the best of condition because they didn't have time to repair it. They had cars that they pulled out of World War I." There was not even a seat for Jim. A conductor let him spend evenings in the dining car after it closed. But the railroads "did a tremendous job keeping things moving with the barest of essentials."

From San Francisco, Jim traveled to Hawaii, where he was assigned to the 90th Naval Construction Battalion, or Seabees (from "C.B." for Construction Battalion). The Navy sent Jim to the Army's two-week-long land mine disposal school. Jim's commander then sent him back to lead a squad of fifteen men in training. The school had a fake graveyard with crosses for soldiers "killed" during training. "I had more crosses than anybody. I was killed three times," he said, laughing.

In January 1945, Jim's construction battalion received orders to ship out to Iwo Jima. While his battalion would have many jobs, the first order of business was to clear construction sites of land mines. "Before we went ashore, I canvassed the fifteen guys in my squad," Jim said. "Anyone who wants to opt out, can. Fourteen of them opted out. I was left with one man who had been trained and fourteen eager young men who had not. Most Seabees were mature and experienced men in their twenties and thirties. When they started, they were interested. When they got there, I could understand [them not wanting to defuse bombs]."

When the 90th Construction Battalion off-loaded on Iwo Jima, twenty-three days after the invasion, the island was not yet secure, so he and his men had to wait in a temporary camp for another twelve days. At sunrise on that twelfth day, March 26, 1945, 280 Japanese made a last, desperate, banzai attack on the southerly portion of Iwo Jima, where Jim and his construction battalion were camped.

"I was awakened shortly after sunrise by the sound of distant gunfire and explosives, but paid little heed, because such disturbances were common throughout most nights," Jim recalled. The gunfire and explosives drew nearer and grew louder until finally subsiding. A few minutes later, Jim was rousted out of bed by his commanding officer. Armed only with .45 pistols and carbine rifles, Jim and his commanding officer set out to investigate. Two of their guards had been killed by saber slashes. Two Japanese soldiers had infiltrated their compound before killing themselves by holding hand grenades against their stomachs.

Eighteen of the Japanese soldiers in this last banzai attack were captured and the rest were killed. Forty-four Americans were killed and 119 wounded. Two of the dead Americans were enlisted Seabees from Jim's battalion.

With Iwo Jima now secure, Jim's battalion set out to do their jobs. Jim had many heart-stopping moments as he and his squad deactivated land mines and other explosives, including bombs, shells and grenades, which, as Jim ruefully pointed out, had not been included in his land mine training.

"The first time I ever deactivated a hand grenade . . . there's only one thing you can do is pick it up and screw the top off so it can't go off. The first time I did that, I was a little nervous," he said, adding that he mistakenly picked it up with an empty munitions tube instead of his bare hands. The hand grenade immediately fell out of the tube onto the ground. "My heart jumped. From then on, I had no problems."

Another time, he came across a sixteen-inch shell that had not exploded. "We had to get rid of it," he said, "so we wrapped a rope around it and started dragging it down the road." He did not get far before some Army bomb experts "hailed us down, came over and started waving their arms." The Army's bomb disposal unit carefully lifted the shell into their truck and drove off. One of their unit explained to Jim that there were wires inside. If the shell bounced around and the wire connected, it would explode. "I didn't know that," Jim said ruefully.

At a work site on the beach, a bulldozer hit a two hundred pound boat mine which exploded. A piece of the bulldozer blade flew between Jim and another guy, barely missing them. The bulldozer operator was severely injured and was evacuated.

"I can remember taking a bomb out one time. It was in the hospital area. It was sticking out of the ground. There wasn't anybody around to take care of it," he said. "The only thing I could do was drag it out of there. So, I had a truck with a winch on the front of it. I drove that truck up fairly close to the bomb, took the rope out, wrapped it around the bomb, and hooked on it. I got on that truck and got down behind the motor and operated the winch and pulled it right out. It didn't go off."

"You do things like this," Jim said. "You're sort of hardened, but you don't become complacent." Jim still takes great pride in the fact that not a single member of his squad was injured despite their quick training, adding that he lectured them constantly about not becoming complacent.

Another unpleasant but necessary job that Jim and his squad had to do was to help the Marines flood Japanese soldiers out of caves. The Marines would first try to convince the Japanese soldiers to come out, but, if they refused, would ask Jim's squad to rig up some pumps and wash them out. Jim recalled waiting by the entrance of a cave as some Marines tried to talk a group of Japanese soldiers out, when a Japanese hand grenade came rolling out.

"We disappeared as fast as possible," he said. The grenade did not explode, and the Marines and Jim's squad turned on the pumps. "That was the end of it."

Jim had other responsibilities, including installing freshwater storage tanks and evaporators to turn salt water into fresh water to be used by the island hospital.

After six months on Iwo Jima, Jim's construction battalion was assigned to the occupation of Japan. He was promoted to lieutenant junior grade and spent another six months building facilities for the American forces. They westernized Japanese facilities, such as replacing Japanese squat pots with western bathrooms. Jim worked closely with local authorities to find locations for housing American civilians.

Through this work, he got to know some of the local Japanese very well, even spending weekends as a guest in their homes.

"I learned to love Japan," he said. "And I learned to like the Japanese people. From the time of actually shooting at them, trying to kill them, helping to drown them on Iwo, looking at them as animals, and then looking at them as human beings was a transition that a lot of military people go through. It's amazing.

"When you're in the field, and your buddy is killed by someone out there who shot him, that guy out there isn't a human being anymore," he explained. "You become a different person. This is exactly what happens. That's why some military people today who come home have a hard time. It does something to you."

After the war, Jim returned to Colorado, working in Denver as a consulting engineer on highway bridges. He briefly worked for the Oregon Insurance Rating Bureau, inspecting industries for fire risk, before returning to graduate school in Colorado.

After a professor offered to arrange an interview with the chief engineer of the Denver and Rio Grande Railroad, Jim agreed to apply and was hired, despite his mother's misgivings. "My mother always told me not to work for a railroad because Dad had," he said.

Jim was promoted extremely rapidly, from trackman to assistant foreman after a few days, then to assistant engineer after a week or so, then to assistant supervisor and supervisor. But he did not like the constant relocation of headquarters on a large railroad. When the Maine Central Railroad broke away from the Boston Railroad, he heard about it, applied, and was hired in 1953 as Engineer of Structures. Jim was headquartered in Portland and did not have to constantly relocate. "It was just what I wanted," he said.

At Maine Central's Portland office, one floor below Jim, a woman named Vaun Dole was working in the president's office. They met, fell in love, and were married in 1957. Vaun soon left Maine Central, deciding to stay home and raise their son and daughter. Their son served four years in the Army in the 1980's and their daughter is a civil engineer, like Jim.

Jim retired from Maine Central in 1984 after serving nineteen years as chief engineer. He had also stayed in the Naval Reserves for forty years, retiring in the 1980's as a full commander.

In both his military and railroad lives, he learned the value of making a decision. Oftentimes, more experienced people would come to him, looking for a decision. He learned how to get information from them, asking them about the pros and cons and alternatives so he could make the final decision. "When he got through telling you what you needed to know, you knew what to do, if you trusted the guy," he said.

"The important thing is a definitive decision," Jim explained. "Sometimes, it's got to be the right decision, but, a lot of times, the difference between the best way and the next best way is not much difference. Somebody wants a decision and when you make a decision, things happen. They get done."

Relocating from Colorado to Maine was easy, Jim said, adding that he loves Maine. Whether in the Navy or at Maine Central, he has always valued doing what he loves in a place that he loves. Other concerns, like money, are less important. Jim did not even ask his salary at Maine Central until after he had accepted the job.

"There are three things in life," he said. "I wanted a job I enjoy to do. I wanted . . . to be working in a place that I wanted to live. And I wanted enough money to have a way to do it. Money is down on number three."

6

VAUN (DOLE) BORN

Be a Joiner

For Vaun Dole, her World War II service in the WAVES, the all-women division of the U.S. Navy (an acronym for "Women Accepted for Volunteer Emergency Service") was part of a lifelong commitment to joining and helping her family and community.

Vaun was born on September 8, 1923. She grew up on Washington Avenue in Portland in a home six generations of her family had owned since 1791, three minutes from her current home on Brook Street in Westbrook. After attending a one-room schoolhouse down the street from her home, she attended Lincoln Junior High School, then Deering High School, then Westbrook Junior College (now part of the University of New England). "We all went to school somewhere on Stevens Avenue for years, all through junior high, high school and college, too."

Vaun attended a three-year program at Westbrook Junior to learn how to teach business classes to high school or college students, "which I never did." As she finished her time at Westbrook College in 1944, Vaun realized that she did not want to teach business. And, "I wanted to help out in the war situation."

She enlisted in the Navy in September 1944 and reported for duty on December 15, 1944. Her parents were not nervous about their only child enlisting, but "[m]y mother was sort of quiet about the whole thing, but then she got active in the [Deering Navy Mothers' Club]. My mother was a joiner when it came to things like that." Vaun's mother became president of the Deering Navy Mothers' Club and took snacks and cigarettes to naval hospitals in Portsmouth during the war.

Vaun took the train to Hunter College in the Bronx for six to eight weeks of initial training. "The first thing I remember, we heard this clop, clop, clop of hooves outside. This was in the Bronx. It was a milk wagon horse. They were still delivering milk that way in New York City."

After her initial training, Vaun attended yeoman school at Oklahoma A&M. In the Navy, yeomen perform administrative and clerical duties. "Going to Oklahoma was the farthest away I had ever been from home," she said. "I remember being on a train at night and you could see forever across those plains. I said: 'oh my God, it is so flat out here.'" Vaun also recalled the pink dust that settled over everything and made for spectacular sunrises and sunsets. The weather was also much different from Maine's. Vaun recalled spying a tornado in the distance "and nobody seemed the least bit excited about it."

When Vaun graduated from yeoman school, the Navy assigned her to the District Intelligence Office in Boston, next to North Station. Vaun was a little disappointed to be transferred to a city she already knew well. "I didn't see the world after all," she said.

In the DIO, Vaun helped file and keep track of records of investigations of naval personnel. Most famously, the DIO helped investigate people involved in the Manhattan Project, but Vaun says that her office did not know what the Manhattan Project was until after the atomic bombs were dropped on Hiroshima and Nagasaki.

Even though the city was familiar, Vaun met women from all over. She lived in a former residential hotel near the capital. "It was the best place in the world to live, people told me later, because it was not on a naval base," she said. "You lived out in the city and you had more freedoms." Vaun also enjoyed socializing at the "Buddies' Club" on Boston Common, a block or so from where she lived on Charles Street. "Living in Boston, that was fairly agreeable and we had good food," she said. Vaun also recalls touring a captured Nazi submarine.

Vaun was later assigned to the Navy's Recreation Department, also in Boston, where she mailed bulletins to various bases around New England informing them of entertainment in their area. She and other members of the Recreation Department also had to make hotel reservations for officers in Boston. "That wasn't exactly the most challenging job," she said.

But there was no room for error. One of her co-workers commuted to work from her home in New Hampshire, and was not very familiar with Boston. A naval officer needed his luggage delivered to the Copley Plaza Hotel, but the co-worker delivered the luggage to the wrong hotel. When she got home, her mother said that someone from her office had called, wanting to know where the luggage was. "We never saw that girl again," Vaun said. "I never dared to ask what ever happened to her."

In 1945, the Navy offered Vaun a promotion to yeoman first class if she stayed in another year, which she did, leaving the Navy in August 1946, after two years of active service. Vaun stayed in the reserves in South Portland for another six years, for a total of eight years of active and reserve military service.

After returning home, Vaun completed her senior year and graduated from the University of Maine at Orono. She did not want to teach business and so went into Portland on Middle Street, "knocking on doors, looking for jobs." She worked at Canal Bank for five years, then at the Maine Central Railroad, as a clerk and stenographer in the president's office. Vaun's father and mother had both worked at the railroad.

A few years after she began working at Maine Central, the railroad hired a new Engineer of Structures, named Jim Born, who worked a floor above Vaun. They met and fell in love and were married in 1957. They moved to a house on Brook Street and have lived there ever since.

Vaun soon left Maine Central, deciding to stay home and raise their son and daughter. She became very active in their Sunday School, Bluebirds, Campfire, Cub Scouts, and several other activities. Vaun also served thirty-six years on the board of directors for the Eunice Frye Home, a home for senior women in Portland. She was the organization's treasurer for thirty-two years. Jim and Vaun's son served four years in the Army in the 1980s and their daughter is a civil engineer, like Jim.

Vaun has been actively involved in preserving Westbrook history, collecting photographs, posters and correspondence of her war years into a notebook which she has shared with the Westbrook Historical Society. She has also donated her naval jacket to the historical society. Vaun is the past-president of the Westbrook Historical Society and authored *100 Years of Westbrook Mayors*. Vaun also wrote a history of the Eunice Frye Home.

Looking back on her life, Vaun connected her military service to her community service and all of her children's activities, saying she was a "joiner" like her mother had been. "With me, it was being involved in the community," said Vaun, who ran for the Westbrook School Board, served as Ward Five warden for elections for years, and also was the president of her alumnae class from Westbrook College. "You feel good about doing and getting involved."

7

ROBERT GUITARD

Travel and Learn About Other Cultures

World War II ended before Robert Guitard had a chance to fight, but his time in Italy overseeing a prisoner of war camp and his travels through Europe in the immediate aftermath of the war taught him the importance of traveling and learning about other cultures. Only by understanding each other can countries avoid war.

Robert's parents had already lost three children by the time they left New Brunswick, Canada, for what they hoped would be a better life in Washington State. On their way to Washington, Robert's family visited his aunt in Westbrook, who convinced them to stay, and her husband found Robert's father a job in S. D. Warren's carpentry department. "He was there his whole career," Robert said. "He loved S. D. Warren."

Robert's parents had nine more children: five sons and four daughters. Robert was the youngest. It wasn't until after his mother's death that Robert learned that she had never been able to read. "I used to see her in the morning with the paper," he said. "She never told us that she couldn't read. I didn't know until after she passed away. She'd hold the paper and look at the pictures. She was a marvelous woman. Oh God, twelve children, just a marvelous woman. I still miss her."

Born in 1927, Robert was fourteen when the Japanese attacked Pearl Harbor on December 7, 1941. He and a friend were exploring the Desert of Maine. "Nobody knew of Pearl Harbor," he said. "Took awhile to sink in."

Four years later, when Robert was a senior at Westbrook High School, he was drafted into the Army, but was allowed to graduate before being shipped off to Fort Devens, Massachusetts, for basic training. Robert recalled seeing many German prisoners of war at Fort Devens before he traveled to Alabama for seventeen weeks of infantry training.

Two of his older brothers were already serving. Edward served on a PT boat in the "smoke invasion" off Calais, France, where the Allies successfully diverted German attention away from Normandy by faking an invasion at Calais. Edward also served in Italy, Africa and the South Pacific. Raymond served in Italy as a nurse in the 5th Army, 45th Division. Raymond was assigned to participate in the Japanese invasion, until Japan surrendered after the United States dropped atomic bombs on Hiroshima and Nagasaki.

Robert was training as a flamethrower and, like Raymond, was going to invade Japan. He had almost finished training when the United States dropped the atomic bombs. "No one knew what an atomic bomb was," he said, "but we knew it was a big bomb and within a couple of days, we knew that it was going to save our lives because we wouldn't have to go. We were very happy. They told us that a million of us wouldn't make it through the invasion. The Japanese had the citizenry ready to defend their homeland."

Instead, in December 1945, Robert sailed on an army transport to Naples, Italy, where he was assigned to help repatriate 20,000 German and Austrian prisoners of war being held in Prisoner of War Enclosure #339 in Pisa, Italy. Robert did not receive any training on how to handle the POW's. The Army was "just anxious to get the thing done with and get us back home," he said.

Robert had studied typing at Westbrook High School and so was put in charge of notifying the International Red Cross of the identities of the POW's so the IRC could contact their families.

During the year that he worked in the POW encampment in Pisa, Robert got to know many of the Austrian and German prisoners. "The Wermacht [regular German Army], they were just drafted guys like I was," he said. "They were okay. They were very anxious to get back to their homeland."

Two Germans worked for him. One spoke perfect English and the other spoke none, but they all offered any skill they had as a reason to get out of the enclosure, even for a brief time. "We had experts in everything imaginable" among the Germans, Robert said. "They'd do anything to get outside the enclosure," including playing in small bands, giving haircuts, or shining shoes.

In return, "[w]e treated them well. We gave them smoking tobacco and all the stewed beef that they wanted and let them play volleyball." Robert also learned a lot of German, like how to say: "no smoking in the hall," which he remembers to this day.

The SS troops were another matter. "They were belligerent," Robert said. "They'd try to protest by not getting a haircut, so we'd give them a haircut. We'd take it all off."

The Italians were starving because the Germans had taken all of their food. "Kids would come up to our mess area with spoons and dip in our garbage pans," he said. "They were starving to death. Their mothers and fathers, the same way. It was sad to see it. The Germans just raped the country, took everything including their food. War is hell."

But, in the aftermath of the hell, came a lot of opportunities for this Westbrook boy to see Europe and learn about many different cultures. "After the war ended in Europe, the Army opened up all these different things for the troops," he said. "But the guys who had actually fought the war, they wanted to get home. So guys like me who came over after the hostilities ended, these opportunities were there. So, I went to Switzerland twice, to Paris twice. I went to Rome twice. When I went to Paris, I didn't have to spend a penny. The Army had hotels in different places just for the troops. As long as you had a pass from your unit, you could go to these places and it didn't cost you a penny."

Robert stayed in the late Italian dictator Benito Mussolini's palace, swimming in his pool that was nearly a football field long and surrounded by statues of Ancient Greek gods. He even had a meeting with Pope Pius XII in his chambers along with six American and four Polish soldiers.

These opportunities sparked a lifelong love of traveling for Robert. But first, he had to begin his postwar life. Robert finished his tour in December 1946 and sailed into New York harbor on Christmas Eve on a Liberty ship made in South Portland. "What a sight that was," he recalled. New York "was all lit up and when we got by the Statue of Liberty, the Army had a band playing for us. It was nice. I remember that very, very well."

Robert was discharged on January 7, 1947, and went to Gray's Business College on the G.I. Bill. Two years later, he graduated, went to work for Armour & Company in Biddeford, and married Geraldine Meggison, his high school sweetheart. Robert worked as a financial controller for a series of insurance companies in Maine, Massachusetts and New York, at one point buying a fifty-acre home outside Utica, New York. Geraldine worked for Manpower as a secretary and was even voted Miss Manpower for the Commonwealth of Massachusetts.

Robert and Geraldine have four sons. One served in the Army, one in the Navy and one in the Marines. The fourth is a respiratory therapist. They also have three grandchildren. After spending years working in Massachusetts and New York, they were excited to return to their hometown of Westbrook

"We always knew that we'd always come back to Maine," Robert said. "Maine is our life."

But over their lives, sparked by Robert's experiences during World War II, Robert and Geraldine have traveled far beyond Westbrook. "We've traveled all over the world," Robert said. "Russia, Estonia, Finland, Norway, Sweden, Denmark, Jamaica, Bermuda." Fifty years after he served in Pisa, Robert returned to Italy with Geraldine, exploring the country from top to bottom; from Lake Como in the north to Sorrento in the south. They tried, but were not able to find, where Prisoner of War Enclosure #339 had been located in Pisa.

"We've been all over," Robert said, proudly.

"Being in the service, I learned to get along with people," Robert said. "You have to get along with people, you're living so close to each other." Even his interactions with the captured Germans and Austrians were valuable because enemies, over time, can become allies. "In the 40's, just the word 'Jap' after Pearl Harbor, I never thought it would turn around the way it has," Robert said. "That's a good lesson."

But the key to understanding other cultures, according to Robert, is to interact with them; to meet the people and get to know them, like he has done his entire life.

"I'm not good at putting my feelings into words," he said, "but we're all made by Jesus Christ, the Lord. It's so silly to be biased against anybody else. We're no better than the next person. If we learn to get along with each other, the world will be better off."

8

ARTHUR AND BILL CURRIER
Recognize the Value of Other Cultures

For many Maine residents, World War II was the moment that the world opened up to them, changing them forever. Growing up in Westbrook, Arthur (born 1925) and Bill Currier (born 1926), had never met people from different parts of America, particularly African-Americans. "I was very innocent and naïve," Arthur said. "I never hardly ever left Westbrook when I was a kid. But when I got around to see people from different areas of the country . . . it's an experience. It's good in a way. It enlightens you a little bit."

Arthur grew up in Westbrook, playing football and basketball for Westbrook High School. When Arthur enlisted in the Navy, his younger brother, Bill, did too. "There were two reasons I entered the service," Bill said, "my brother, Arthur, did and I did everything he did and I was big enough, old enough, and my country needed me and I was going."

Both men enlisted as soon as they could after Pearl Harbor; Arthur in February 1943 and Bill the next month. "When we went in, you didn't have to twist anyone's arm," Arthur explained. "It was after Pearl Harbor. Practically everyone volunteered to go in."

After basic training, both men were stationed on different destroyers in the Pacific. Arthur was on fire prevention below deck and Bill was a radar operator. Both men saw plenty of action in the Pacific. In the Philippines, when Arthur's ship, the USS *Connor*, and another destroyer intercepted Japanese transports trying to island-hop, Japanese planes bombed his ship. "Close enough that we didn't want any more of it," he recalled. "It was a lucky ship." In Guam, a Japanese sub fired torpedoes at his ship, but missed. At Iwo Jima, the USS *Connor* bombed many different islands, supporting the strike force, and fought off kamikazes.

Bill's first combat was in the Marshall Islands in early 1944, where he found himself stationed at a gun instead of the radar. His destroyer bombarded the islands. It was "an old time movie," he said, with ships lined up, firing and island forces firing back, but his ship did not get hit. His destroyer participated in battles in the Mariana Islands, New Guinea, Truk, and the Philippines, but the action got more intense the closer he got to Japan. His ship was ahead of the rest of the fleet, serving as early warning radar. They were all alone when 250 Japanese aircraft descended from the skies. "And the first thing they see is you," Bill said. But his ship was not hit. It did shoot down five kamikazes.

In the Philippines, he was at battle stations for four straight days, fighting off kamikazes, and sleeping standing up at his radar station. His destroyer provided anti-submarine cover for the invading forces. Once the American forces landed, his destroyer provided gunnery support, firing on Japanese pill boxes. A sister ship was torpedoed and sunk a half-mile away. He can still see the dying men swimming through the burning oil. At Iwo Jima, two of their four destroyers were sunk.

Combat was intense, particularly in the moments just after the guns fire and the sailors were below deck, waiting to see if the attacking Japanese planes made it through to the ship.

"All those goddamned planes in the air and you pray that they don't go for you," Bill said. "You don't know why they pick one ship over another. We were both lucky. I had a good ship. A lucky ship. They could have picked our ship, but they didn't." By the time Bill's ship returned to America, the guns had to be replaced because they had been fired so many times.

Arthur and Bill also survived the deadly typhoons that tossed the destroyers like toy ducks in a bathtub. "When a typhoon crosses the Pacific . . . the ocean waves are sixty feet tall," Bill explained. "In one convoy, three ships rolled over. When you roll over, there's nothing to do. You're trapped and you swear to God that it's never going to right itself. I once spent eight hours like that. I was absolutely convinced that I was going to die. . . . That was the scariest thing, by far, that I ever went through, and I went through two of them. The first one was bad. The second one was horrible." Their parents even heard a mistaken report that Bill's ship had sunk, and had to wait a full day for the correction.

After enlisting one month apart, the brothers were discharged one month apart: Bill in February and Arthur in March 1946.

In the service, Arthur and Bill noticed how some sailors treated the African-American sailors poorly. "There were about half a dozen on the ship," Arthur said. "They lived by themselves. Didn't mingle or eat with the others. It wasn't right." On Bill's ship, a group of sailors refused to talk to him after he ate a tin of fudge prepared by an African-American soldier. "What the hell do I care what color his skin is?" Bill asked. "He's a nice guy. I'll tell you something about those black guys. When combat started, they were on the same guns as the white guys. So they did their part." Added Arthur: "Thank God that's not so bad anymore. There's a lot of people still fighting the Civil War." Both brothers take the same open-minded approach to other cultures. "My advice to people is: think, think, think," Bill said. "We've got to stop being as prejudiced as we are. Other cultures are as good as ours. We have to recognize that."

Both men carried these lessons with them as they returned to Westbrook and went to work for S. D. Warren. Bill managed quality control and technical services at the mill. Arthur has been married for fifty-nine years to his high school girlfriend, Mariette Labrecque; Bill for sixty-four years to the love of his life, Janet Aube. Bill and Janet raised three sons, their oldest serving as vice admiral in the Coast Guard. Arthur and Mariette raised three daughters and one son. Bill also served on the Westbrook City Council in the early 1960s.

"Good life," Arthur said. "I'm lucky. God's been good to me."

9

JEAN MARC DESJARDINS

Know the Value of a Good Friend

Every soldier speaks of the value of a good buddy, a comrade-in-arms during war. Jean Marc Desjardins found his in a fellow bomb disposal technician nicknamed Puddinghead.

Jean Marc was born in 1920 in St. Andre, Canada. His father worked in his uncle's factory and his mother took care of the family and home. When the uncle's factory burned down, Jean Marc's family moved to Lewiston, Maine, so his father could find work as a contractor.

Jean Marc was two years old when he moved to Lewiston with his parents and older sister, Theresa. His father became an American citizen, but the two children remained Canadian citizens when Lewiston city officials mistakenly told their father that the children would automatically become citizens when he did. When Jean Marc enlisted in the U.S. Army, he was still a Canadian and shipped out before he could switch.

Even though they moved to America, Jean Marc's family found a familiar home in Lewiston's French-Canadian community. But Jean Marc was surprised to find that many of the neighbor children did not speak English despite having been born in America. His father insisted that his children learn English immediately in order to assimilate into their new country and sent them to St. Patrick's, the Irish school, rather than to the French-Canadian school. While his French would come in handy during World War II, Jean Marc was always glad that his father made him learn English when he was young.

After graduating from Lewiston High School, Jean Marc went to work as a clerk for Day's Jewelry Store in Lewiston, and became very close to the owners, the Davidsons, who gave him a beautiful watch when he enlisted and wrote to him often while he was overseas.

On June 17, 1942, Jean Marc enlisted in the U.S. Army. The Canadian Army had drafted him, since he was still a Canadian citizen, but he immediately applied for American citizenship and was sent to Fort Devens, Massachusetts, for basic training and then to the Aberdeen Proving Grounds for bomb disposal school. Jean Marc had wanted to be a paratrooper, but the Army rejected him because of a heart condition and instead trained him to defuse bombs, which, apparently, would not affect his heart condition.

It was while at Aberdeen that he met his combat buddy, Leo Kloda of Buffalo, New York. Kloda, nicknamed Puddinghead (although Jean Marc no longer can remember why he got that nickname), was training to be a technical corporal in the bomb disposal intelligence squad, like Jean Marc. While Jean Marc was thin with a French accent and was a devout Catholic, Puddinghead was stocky with a thick Polish accent, and refused to go to church, but the two bonded. After both finished training at Aberdeen, they were shipped together to Harlow, England, for more train-ing in bomb disposal with the British Army's Royal Engineers.

The two friends saw plenty of action right away, defusing Ger-man bombs dug deep in the British clay and chalk. German bombs were more advanced than American ones at that time, Jean Marc said, with sophisticated electrical fuses instead of the American striker mechanisms. Because the chalk and clay were so permeable, the German bombs would often dig down as deep as ninety feet without exploding. Jean Marc and the other members of his squad would have to climb down into the hole with the bomb and attempt to defuse it, aware that the wrong movement could set off a booby trap or trigger the bomb.

Before climbing into the hole, Jean Marc and his squad mem-bers would give their dog tags to someone above. He would say every movement before he did it, to avoid making mistakes. Jean Marc recalls dropping into a hole with his commanding officer to find one of the biggest German bombs he had ever seen. They could hear the timer ticking. If it stopped, they knew they had only three seconds before the bomb would explode. To defuse the bomb, they had to remove two fuses. Because the fuses were electrical, they had to discharge the electricity in order to remove them. As the timer ticked away, Jean Marc and the CO placed a Coleman stove and steamer on top of the fuses to discharge the electricity. After successfully defusing the bomb, Jean Marc and his CO were so shaky that they could not climb out of the hole.

While training in England, Jean Marc saw many tragedies. The gas from German bombs that exploded deep underground would slowly bubble up through the clay, forming a pocket, just under the surface. Anyone walking across would fall through and be killed by the gas.

To avoid the bombs, many English people hid in the subways. Jean Marc saw women and children sleeping on the landings in the Liverpool Street station. When the station flooded and water covered the electrical rail, everyone was electrocuted. "It was terrible," Jean Marc said.

For D-Day, Jean Marc's squad was assigned to the Army's 7 Corps, the spearhead of the First Army, under the command of Generals Lawton Collins and Omar Bradley.

As Jean Marc landed on Utah Beach, under the withering fire, he was paralyzed with fear, unable to force himself to do his assignment, which was to blow a pillbox. Just then, he heard someone shout: "Oh God! Don't let me die. I'll go to mass every Sunday." It was Puddinghead. "I thought, if he's scared, I have a right to be scared, too. That woke me up. So I did my job and blew up the pillbox."

Decades later, Jean Marc's grandson, a history teacher at Gorham High School, took his children to Utah Beach. The remains of the pillbox that Jean Marc destroyed were still there.

After making it off Utah Beach, Puddinghead asked Jean Marc to take him to Father Gleason, the chaplain, which he did. After that, Puddinghead "was a good Christian" and regularly attended mass.

Puddinghead was also a funny guy who loved a good drink, particularly the apple brandy brewed in Normany, called Calvados. During a brief lull in the fighting in Normandy, Jean Marc was surprised to see Puddinghead strolling between the hedgerows, leading two pigs on leashes. Jean Marc yelled at him to get down before he was shot by a German sniper, but Puddinghead, full of Calvados, refused. When Jean Marc asked him what he was doing with the pigs, Puddinghead said: "I thought we'd have pork chops!"

Puddinghead would soon save Jean Marc's life. After being among the first American troops to cross the Siegfried Line into Germany and surviving devastating fighting outside of Aachen, Germany (where Jean Marc and Puddinghead had to defuse bombs caught in the camouflage netting), their squad was ordered to Belgium to participate in the Battle of the Bulge. As they arrived, some soldiers in American uniforms approached them. The soldiers had German accents. Jean Marc and the other Americans believed that the soldiers were from the Midwest, which had many German immigrant communities. But they were really Nazi soldiers who had stolen American uniforms.

They opened fire, killing fifteen American soldiers and taking hundreds prisoner, including Jean Marc, Puddinghead and another member of their squad, Paul Hinton. The Germans hid the prisoners in a nearby barn, but separated the three members of the bomb squad, thinking they had useful information.

The Germans took their clothes except for their socks and cap, despite the freezing conditions. Puddinghead knew that they had to escape, saying "they're going to put us through hell. We've got to get out."

Puddinghead still had a pack of cigarettes. He told Jean Marc and Paul Hinton to be ready, and offered a cigarette to the German guard. When he accepted it, Puddinghead grabbed the guard's helmet, which was strapped tightly under his chin, and twisted it violently, snapping the guard's neck. Then, Puddinghead, Jean Marc and Hinton dove out of a small window into a pile of manure.

"That manure was hot," Jean Marc recalled, but the heat quickly evaporated as the three men trudged in just their socks and cap through the snow in the coldest winter Europe had seen in decades. Jean Marc had three pairs of wool socks on, but his feet quickly went numb. When one of his legs stopped working, he told the others to go on without him. They refused.

When they finally found a roving American patrol and were taken to a field hospital, they spotted a number of soldiers who had been captured and imprisoned in the barn, but were now wounded. Shortly after the three men had escaped, a French plane bombed the barn. If they had not escaped, they might have been killed. Puddinghead, Jean Marc and Hinton received the Bronze Star for their heroics.

Not long after that, the war ended and Jean Marc's squad was transferred to occupation duty in Berlin.

Berlin was "a lot of fun" for Jean Marc. The fighting was finished and he had a chance to meet German citizens. He even spent a month at a university in Berlin, learning German.

Jean Marc's language skills played an important role in his service, landing him the role of unofficial interpreter while they were in France, and drawing praise from Generals Collins and Bradley themselves. While trying to buy potatoes in Normandy, Jean Marc discovered that the French the farmers spoke was very similar to his French Canadian. When his CO learned that Jean Marc could understand the local French, he told General Collins. After the 7 Corps captured St.-Lo, General Bradley was trying to talk to the mayor, but his interpreter could not understand the local official. General Collins sent Jean Marc to General Bradley.

Jean Marc discovered that Bradley's interpreter was speaking "Parisian" French. "If you're speaking Parisian French, you're not speaking the right French," Jean Marc said. "You need to speak grammatical French."

As he listened to the mayor, Jean Marc realized why the interpreter was having such a struggle. The mayor stuttered. As he grew more frightened by the Americans, his stutter grew worse.

"I said, 'sir, they don't teach that at Harvard: French stuttering,'" Jean Marc said. Bradley laughed and told Jean Marc to continue as the interpreter. "You're doing a good job," the general said. "Keep it up."

Jean Marc was discharged in November 1946. When he returned to Lewiston, the Davidsons wanted him to open a Day's Jewelry store in Rockland, but he wanted to go into insurance, like his sister, and so he went to work selling insurance for Boston Mutual Insurance Company. He then went to work for his cousin's company, Central Distributors, selling Schlitz, where he stayed for forty years.

Jean Marc dated a woman for a while, but when she did not want to raise children Catholic, Jean Marc, always a devout Catholic, broke up with her. He remained a bachelor until 1997, when he married Yvette Fournier, a friend of his sister's whom he had known since childhood. "My father was so happy I was marrying her," Jean Marc said. "She is a wonderful person." Yvette volunteered at St. Mary's Hospital in Lewiston and at the senior center.

Jean Marc never had children of his own, but adopted Yvette's four daughters and nineteen grandchildren. After waiting so long to have a family, Jean Marc thanks God for them and plans to enjoy them a good bit longer, pointing out that his father lived to be 106 years old and a 108-year-old great-aunt still lives in Quebec.

His great-aunt tells him: "Jean, don't worry about things. The Good Lord will take care of you."

Just like a good friend always does.

10

LUCIEN "LOU" MATHIEU

Enjoy Life Even When It's Difficult or Painful

Lucien, or Lou (or "Fiddling Lou"), Mathieu lived life to the fullest despite being shot at as a World War II bomber pilot over Germany and surviving many crashes. He always enjoyed a drink, a good fight, pretty ladies, and a lot of fiddling. Much later in life, Lou remained an optimist with a zest for life despite spending every day in the Barron Center with his wife, Marie, who was suffering from Alzheimer's. Lou spent the last three years as a patient at the Barron's Center, in the same room as his wife, and when he passed in 2011, he was surrounded by his family playing his favorite fiddling tunes.

Lou was born on July 11, 1923, in Winslow, Maine. His father had come down from Bowshead, Quebec, to chop wood and met Lou's mother. The oldest of nine children (he had five brothers and three sisters), Lou graduated from Winslow High School in 1941 and immediately joined the Air Force.

"The minute I graduated, I went to Bangor to join the Air Force," he said.

After basic training, Lou learned to be a radio operator. But it was on a flight to Boise, Idaho, his first time in a plane, that he discovered his wartime calling. The plane crashed. Lou was the only survivor, spending forty-five days in a hospital.

"I said to myself, hell, if I am going to crash, I want to fly the Goddamned thing. So I took the test and passed it good," he said. "So they shipped me down to Texas, Amarillo, to learn to be a pilot."

From 1942 to 1945, Lou served as a bomber pilot, flying B-24 Liberators over Germany and other Nazi-occupied territories. His first bombing run was over occupied Belgium. Many of his missions were over Germany's industrial and heavily defended Ruhr Valley or over Berlin.

"They used to shoot flack at us, we called it, and it would blow open and bust open, and they shot a lot of planes down," Lou said. "That is why I was over there so soon. And I also had fighters, but the [German] fighters were pretty well ruined after a while because we ruined their gas bases and stuff."

Lou returned from one bombing run with 180 holes in his plane. Another time, his engine was knocked off. Lou crashed four more times (after his first outside Boise, Idaho), narrowly missing having to ditch in the English Channel, but was never hurt again. Lou recalled seeing pilots trying to escape doomed aircraft all around him. "Their parachutes open and all of a sudden it goes up straight like that, their chute, you know, and they go down like a bullet, you know, straight down," he said. "They just went like hell. I seen a lot of that."

Lou flew thirty-five missions, but actually volunteered for one additional mission. He was not listed on the flight crew, but flew it just to help out. Lou received the Air Force's Air Medal and a number of other commendations.

Despite all this, Lou "usually had a lot of fun when I was in England."

"I had a lot of fun playing the fiddle in England," he said. "They loved that type of music. I was playing jigs. They liked that, you know. And the girls liked us, too, some of them. The guys didn't like us."

Lou would play at local pubs and even had his name on a mug at one of the pubs and all the free beer he wanted. "So we had good times over there," he said.

In 1945, Lou was discharged and returned home to Winslow, where his family was waiting for him at the train station. That Christmas, Lou met Marie and they were married the following May.

Lou thought about attending Colby College, but went to meat-cutting school instead. "I like to eat good," he explained. "I worked for the A&P and I became the meat manager right off."

Lou was the meat manager for the A&P for twenty years and also helped establish the meat-cutters' union, even serving as its president. But life was not always easy even though the war was over. Lou and his wife, Marie, lost two sons in childbirth before their son, Louis Mathieu, survived. After Louis' successful birth, "We thought we were on our way," but another son died in childbirth before their daughter, Marie, was born.

Despite this pain, Lou continued to embrace life, with his family and his music. Having learned to play the fiddle from his own father and uncle, Lou taught his son and nephew and many others. Over the years, Lou played at Carnegie Hall in New York, on Garrison Keillor's *A Prairie Home Companion*, and on countless stages, radio shows and television programs. Lou was a member of the Katahdin Mountaineers and helped lead the Maine French Fiddlers ensemble. In 1992, he was inducted into the Maine Country Music Hall of Fame.

But, in 2001, Marie was diagnosed with Alzheimer's. Lou spent more and more time, each day, with Marie at the Barron's Center. In 2008, Lou moved into Marie's room to be with her full-time.

"She's got Alzheimer's," Lou said from their room in the Barron's Center. "That is a bad disease. She is not the same woman. I am glad to still have her with me, so I've got to watch over her."

But Lou also brought his fiddle and guitar with him. Even though he could no longer lead the summer fiddling classes like he used to, he could still play the fiddle with his son in his room at the Barron's Center.

On September 4, 2011, Lou passed away in his room with Marie at the Barron's Center, with his family playing some of his favorite fiddling tunes.

11

JIM FINLEY
Use Your Gifts

From an "aptitude for mechanics" to a "gift for numbers," Jim Finley used the gifts he received in his life.

In 1922, Jim was born on a kitchen table in the Windham home in which he lived until his death. His father bought thirty-seven acres of land in Windham with a house and barn for $1,500. "It took him eight years to pay for it," Jim said. His father bought the rest of the family homestead, now totaling sixty-six acres, in 1932, and they raised chickens, cows, horses, pigs and a "little bit of everything."

Jim played basketball and baseball as a boy. After graduating from Windham High School in 1938, he went to work for the Boston Maine Railroad. "Back in those days, between that and S.D. Warren, those were the big employers," Jim said.

He also enrolled at Portland Junior College, wanting to ultimately transfer to the University of Notre Dame for an accounting degree. "That's my gift, if you want to call it that," he said. "I have a real good memory for figures."

But the war "detoured my expectations."

"When I was twenty-one, the Army was looking for me," he said. "But I outfoxed them. I joined the Navy and left a week before I was supposed to join the Army." Jim chose the Navy over the Army because his father had been in the Army in World War I and got "gassed" by the mustard gas.

"We took tests before we were assigned," Jim said. "An aptitude test. From the results of the test, they decided that I had aptitude for mechanics. I used to tear my father's car apart when I was younger, so I knew a little bit about mechanics.

"I was good at mathematics, too, but they selected me for mechanics," he said.

The Navy sent Jim to Newport, Rhode Island, for two months of diesel school, then to Norfolk, Virginia, for advanced diesel school. After graduating, Jim was assigned to an auxiliary patrol craft out of Deer Island, California.

"It was supposed to be an inter-island transport, transporting goods from one island to another," he explained. "I had to wait for the ship to be commissioned. It was being built in the San Francisco Navy Yard. When we finally got the ship launched and had the sea trials, we went to Pearl Harbor. When we got to Pearl Harbor, they loaded us up with 100 tons of dynamite. We took dynamite from Pearl Harbor to Midway Island without an escort. Our only defense was two 35mm guns. But we made it there and back."

But Jim could not stand the APC. "I couldn't stand the diesel fumes in the engine room," he said. "They had no ventilation. And the rocking and rolling. I couldn't hack it so I got off that ship and stayed in Pearl Harbor for a couple weeks. Then they shipped me down to New Hebrides. It took us thirty days to go from Pearl

Harbor to New Hebrides." New Hebrides was an archipelago in the South Pacific east of Australia, now known as Vanuatu.

Jim sailed to New Hebrides on the USS *Kitty Hawk*. Because it was transporting fighter planes, Jim and the other soldiers had to sleep on the deck on cots. "A lot of the Army guys, they got real sick," he said. "Seasick. They couldn't handle it. I was all right. If you're in close quarters, like on the APC, which is a 100-foot boat and you have this big diesel engine that's probably six feet high and twelve feet long and pistons and those diesel fumes and you're rocking and rolling and there's no ventilation, you're bound to get sick."

As soon as he arrived, he was put to work. "The night we got there to New Hebrides, some of my friends were flown up," he said. "They were bombing Funafuti [a coral island on which the Americans had an airbase that they used to defend the Gilbert Islands and Marshall Islands] that night. I went up the next day. We stayed on that island for eighteen months. I was a mechanic. Took care of all the diesel engines and the automobiles and trucks. Anything that needed mechanical services. Refrigeration units."

Jim had not been trained on refrigeration and air conditioning, but "I just figured it out." He had no crew. "I was more or less on my own," he said. "I was a first-class mechanic."

One of the first orders of business was to build refrigeration units for the base the Navy was establishing on Funafuti. "We didn't have any refrigeration for water," Jim said. "They had a canvas sack that would fill up with water. If we wanted anything, we'd have to drink that hot water. That was for a couple weeks. Once we got established, then they got everything refrigerated and we had beer.

"Our food supply was furnished by the Army at that time," he said. "For the first two weeks we were there, we ate dehydrated eggs and dehydrated potatoes. That's all we had. But as the supplies came in, we had a freezer and a refrigerator unit. We had an auxiliary unit that would power the refrigeration units." Once he got the refrigeration up and running, Pan Am flew in their food supplies.

He and the storekeeper were even able to convince the Pan Am crews to pack away some liquor from time to time.

"I really enjoyed it for a while, but after eighteen months, and you never saw anyone but Army or Navy guys . . ." he said, not finishing the thought.

After the New Hebrides, Jim spent a couple months on New Caledonia, taking care of "all the engine work that needed to be done there." Then he was off to Brisbane, Australia. "I never saw any action at all, but I was right behind the action," he said. "I was very fortunate."

But when Jim was transferred to Saipan, he saw the devastation of war first hand. "You ever hear of Suicide Cliff?" he asked. "We lived in tents while we were there. The only thing I had for protection was a knife. They [Japanese citizens and soldiers] were jumping off the cliff right and left, off Suicide Cliff. You didn't sleep very well at nighttime when you first went there, knowing there were plenty of Japanese around."

After leaving Saipan, Jim spent some time on Guam, then was assigned to the Navy base in Kansas City, Missouri, taking care of the ground equipment.

After being discharged in September 1945, Jim wanted to return to school, but once again, life had other plans. "I had wanted to go back to college," he said. "I had started college at what used to be Portland Junior College—it's now the University of Southern Maine—before I went in the service. When I came back, my mother was alone. I'd been away for three years and she had no means of support. So I stayed around and forfeited my chance to go to school on the G.I. Bill. The railroad was waiting for me to come back."

At the Boston Maine Railroad, Jim used his other gift, for mathematics, working as an auditor, checking station accounts, conductors' accounts, and freight bills, until 1962.

A year after returning from World War II, Jim met his wife, Jean, at a dance at the Jack O'Lantern Dance Hall in South Portland. His wife was too young to go to the dance, but, she explained, "my mother knew I was going. I went with my sister, who was older."

"Back in those days, all the big bands used to come," Jim recalled. "Count Basie. Digger Dempsey. Tommy Dorsey. I used to go see them at the pier before the war. You'd get in for a dime."

Jim and Jean were married in 1947 and had seven children. They now have ten grandchildren and five great-grandchildren, most of whom still live in Maine.

Jim left the railroad in 1962 to use his gifts for numbers and mechanics by going into a business where Jim would repair automobiles and his partner would sell them. Two years later, Jim decided to go to work for Blue Cross, making sure that their books balanced. He worked for Blue Cross until 1977, then, once again, used his talent for numbers to run a dog track in New Hampshire. He figured payouts at that track and the racetrack in Scarborough without any help from a computer. He still calculates the payouts for the Skowhegan and Cumberland racetracks. He then worked as office manager for RNS Seafood on the waterfront until 1994, keeping the company's books and paying its bills. When RNS Seafood's founder passed away, Jim inherited some fishing vessels and a tanker/ice breaker. Once again combining his talents for mechanics and mathematics, he began transporting logs from Portland to Iceland in 1995 and importing red fish bait from Iceland to Maine.

Over the years, Jim kept in contact with some of his military buddies, including the storekeeper from Funafuti, holding a reunion in 1980. "If you feel that you'd like to join the service, it's healthy for everybody," he said. You "learn a lot."

One thing Jim learned from his time in the South Pacific is that he hates the heat. "It'd be 120 down in the islands," he said. To this day, Jim refuses to travel to Florida and loves Maine winters, even the shoveling.

His time in the Navy also exposed him to the world and different cultures. "I've been around the world," he said. "If there's something I haven't done, I don't know what it is. But these computers, they bug me."

Instead, Jim was always content to rely on his gifts. They'd gotten him this far.

Sadly, Jim passed away on July 9, 2012, at his home on Finley Road in Windham.

12

HERMAN BOUDREAU

Get a Good Education and Help People

As a soldier and a Maine state trooper, Herman Boudreau never stopped learning and teaching despite never finishing the fifth grade. Born in Waterville on January 20, 1920, Herman spent most of his time working. "When I was a kid growing up," he recalled. "My father, Saturday morning, he'd say you do this, do this, do this, mostly sawing wood all day long. And in the fields, guys played baseball, football. I remembered that always, so I never let my kids work."

Herman worked highway construction from Waterville to Augusta and hauled logs in the winter from Rumford. At the age of seventeen, he joined the Civilian Conservation Corps, working at a girls' camp in Craig, Colorado, building bridges and roads across America and killing rattlesnakes and prairie dogs. "We'd line up and we had a little bag of poison oats that we'd put in the holes where the prairie dogs were. We'd catch the rattlesnakes and cut off the rattles because the government wanted to know how many we killed. And we built roads. Just cut the mountain down for roads and bridges. I liked that experience."

When the Japanese attacked Pearl Harbor on December 7, 1941, Herman was working construction in Waterville. "I did like everybody else. One hundred and seven of us left Waterville that year. There's only three of us left now, out of 107."

"I volunteered [for the U.S. Army] Christmas Day, 1941. I had just entered the National Guard. Of course, all the National Guard people were from Maine," he said. "We went into World War II with Maine people. I remember we were in New Zealand. We had just gotten done eighteen months of fighting in the South Pacific. We lost quite a few people." When reinforcements arrived, "I'm standing there and down the street here comes David Rabinowitz, a neighbor and friend of mine from Waterville."

But before he headed off to war, Herman first went to basic training at Camp Drum, New York, then to infantry training at Fort Benning, Georgia, where he learned hand-to-hand combat, how to use a bayonet, and how to shoot a rifle. Herman also learned how to dig spider holes; "[l]ittle round ones that you just went into so tanks could go over. You got your shoulders down in there."

Herman was a member of G Company, 103rd Infantry, 43rd Division, 2nd battalion, made up mostly of New England men. During training, Herman prepared to deploy to Europe, learning flanking movements that would cover twenty to thirty miles. But instead, he shipped out to the jungles of the South Pacific. "Of course, when you're in a jungle, a flanking movement is twenty to thirty yards."

Crossing the Pacific was rough for the Maine boy. He frequently got seasick below deck and so "borrowed" one of the deck sailors' hats so he could stay on deck.

Despite his seasickness, Herman spent twenty-seven months in the South Pacific based on ships, hopping from island to island, and cleaning out Japanese resistance. Being seasick "stopped after a while when we got out in the open water because it wasn't so rough." When island-hopping, "it was touch and go. I was sick most of the time. It didn't last long. You didn't worry or think about it much. You just kept going on what your mission was."

Herman's first action was at Guadalcanal, where he earned a Bronze Star for his role in removing the last Japanese resistance on three occupied islands and securing an airfield. "There were a few scattered Japanese left. I took seven men . . . and went out in the bush. We chased them out." Herman said he was not nervous. "It seemed like everything came naturally. We were well-trained. We were all anxious. I guess we might have been afraid, but I can't remember. We were anxious to get in there. Of course, they made us think we were superhuman, that we could do anything." After three days, the islands and the airport were secure.

But Herman had been shot in the arm, for which he received the Purple Heart. After he recovered, he was sent to New Caledonia, an island east of Australia, and continued to move island to island, attacking Japanese resistance and securing the islands. On New Georgia, part of the Solomon Islands northwest of Guadalcanal, Herman earned his Silver Star for leading a stranded tank out of the jungle while under fire.

"We never operated with tanks. We never had tanks in our training, but when we were over there in the jungle, all of a sudden, we had three tanks assigned," he said. "They worked in pairs. That was good for us because it made a lot of noise. We were in a foxhole. . . . We got hit." A tank crew accidentally shot two American soldiers, including their sergeant.

"They were very panicky," Herman explained. "They were afraid of anti-tank bombs that [the Japanese] hook on the back. So, one tank took off and went into the jungle. Disappeared. The other two tanks wouldn't move until this one got back. I went into the jungle. There's a telephone behind the tank, but it didn't work. So I took the butt of my rifle. They have a little slit on the turret. They turned it around and they could see me. I kept going 'this way.' All this time, I was being shot at, the tank was. It sounded like firecrackers because they had those .22s. It sounded just like firecrackers. They were hitting that tank and why I didn't get hit, I don't know. I pounded on the tank and he opened it. So he followed me back."

But the danger was not just from enemy fire. Herman was walking backwards through a dense jungle, steps in front of the oncoming tank. "I can always remember the 'great fall,'" he said. "You're in the jungle and if I fell, it would be the end because he couldn't see me. So I finally got him back." He did not know until a year later that he had received a Silver Star.

Herman spent twenty-seven months in the South Pacific, rising to the rank of command sergeant major, the highest rank for a NCO. He was supposed to be in an office, but he could not stay away from the unit. "It was supposed to be mostly paperwork, but I wasn't good at it, so I went out in the field and worked with everybody, trained with everybody, and fought with everybody."

While Herman, as command sergeant major, spent a good bit of his time training others, his lifelong role as a teacher was only beginning.

Herman returned from the South Pacific to California, then took a train home to Maine, where he did not waste any time starting the post-war phase of his life. He took the state police sergeant's exam in the cupola in the Capitol building in Augusta, despite his fear of heights, passed it, and joined the state police six days later, on December 23, 1945.

His first assignment was on a motorcycle, which he knew how to ride, but not how to stop. "I went from Augusta to Jackman," he said. "I wouldn't stop because I'd never ridden a motorcycle." Six months later, they gave him a Chevolet with 200,000 miles on it. "Took me a mile to get going as fast as I could and a mile to stop it. But I shined it up."

Herman was in charge of the Highway Safety Program, and a large part of his job was talking to children about safety. He loved teaching kids. "How eager they are to learn," he said. "It motivates you."

Herman also trained other officers, wrote a newspaper for the state police, and stayed active in the National Guard, training local police, sheriffs and state police at the Maine Criminal Justice Academy on how to respond to riots. In 1965, Herman received the first Trooper of the Year award.

After briefly being recalled to active service during the Berlin Crisis in the 1960s, Herman retired from the state police in 1967. Always one to keep busy, he served as chief of police in Freeport, Maine, and then started a courier service, transporting money for Bath Iron Works, Shaw's and some banks for six years in a "little Studebaker." Herman and his wife of fifty-four years, Nancie, moved to Brooklyn, New York, for two years in the late 1980's and volunteered at a homeless shelter. After returning to Maine, he helped Nancie run the Three Little Bears Nursery School in Brunswick until 2010.

Most of Herman's military friends are gone now, but Herman, who has lived in Brunswick for the last fifty-three years, still has his pennants from each island he landed on and his military side-arm, cleaned and ready. Most importantly, he has a lifetime of lessons learned and taught to others.

And he has shared this dedication to teaching and serving others with his family. His wife, Nancie, ran her nursery school for forty-eight years, even teaching two years while in a wheelchair when she broke her leg in a skiing accident and it did not heal correctly. More than five thousand children attended the nursery school before it closed in 2010, knowing Herman as "Mr. Policeman" or "Pepere." Herman has also instilled this love of learning and of serving others in his four children, including one son who is a police lieutenant in California.

Looking back, Herman said he had learned two important lessons. "First, get a good education. That's number one. Number two, is try to help people. Do everything you can do to help others. That's what I liked more than anything else was doing something for people."

Herman passed away on April 7, 2013.

13

WINNIE (WHALEN) CLEMONS
You Have to Give Before You Can Receive

Winnie Whalen left Lincoln, Maine, to serve in the WAVES ("Women Accepted for Volunteer Emergency Service," which later became the U.S. Naval Women's Reserve), looking for adventure. Even though she was terrified to leave home, and leave Maine, for the first time, she understood that "you've got to give before you can receive." Winnie has spent the rest of her post-war life in Lincoln, living that motto.

Winnie was born on November 23, 1922, in Lincoln. Her father worked in the Lincoln Pulp and Paper Mill, and her mother took care of the home and family: Winnie, her older brother, and three younger sisters. Lincoln "was a close-knit community," Winnie said, where any child could get a band-aid in any house. Winnie was very close to her family, who were protective of her. "I was eight years old before my dad took me down to Main Street," she recalled. And she loved playing baseball. "I hated boys, but I played baseball with them," she said.

After graduating from Mattanawcook High School in Lincoln in 1940, Winnie spent her days working at the local grocery store and then at the paper mill, and her evenings going to dance halls in Mattawamkeag and Lee with her girlfriends. But she wanted more. She wanted to help the war effort and to have some adventures. In June 1942, Winnie enlisted in the WAVES because it was the only service for which she was old enough. She tried to persuade some of her girlfriends to enlist with her, but "I could not find one girl in this town to go with me."

She traveled on the train to Boston to enlist, the first time she had ever left Maine. "I was absolutely scared to death," she said. A man on the train knew her father and sat with her until Portland, which helped calm her nerves. "I was never so pleased to see someone else in my life," she said.

Winnie's parents supported her decision, which made it easier. "They knew I was a wild child," she said. Winnie's older brother later joined the Navy and one of her younger sisters joined the Canadian Army.

From Boston, Winnie traveled to Hunter College in the Bronx for basic training. The WAVES enlistees were kept busy with classwork and training and did not have a lot of time to socialize. "It was strictly strict," she recalled, emphasizing the tightly controlled regimen. "We were there to learn and we had to. I paid attention and kept my mouth shut."

After graduating as a yeoman (in the Navy, yeomen perform administrative and clerical duties), Winnie was assigned to the commissary, or ship's store, in Portland, where she stocked 24 ships with food. She and the other WAVES stayed four to a room at the Eastland Hotel. In their free time, they could explore Portland, but only if accompanied by a man or by at least two other WAVES. Supplying that many ships was hard and challenging, but interesting work.

After one and a half years in Portland, Winnie was assigned to the Brunswick Naval Air Station, where she drove a jeep, carried a gun, and delivered mail to the officers. After a year in Brunswick, the Navy asked if any of the women wanted to serve overseas. Winnie immediately volunteered and was shipped to Ford Island at Pearl Harbor. The island had been in the center of the Japanese attack because of the battleship moorings that surrounded it. Much of the devastation from the Japanese bombs was still apparent, although much had been repaired and built up since the attack. Winnie recalls sitting on the edge of the pier, staring down at the sunken USS *Arizona*.

She was not scared to serve at Pearl Harbor because she had faith that God would protect her. "I had a very strong faith and I knew God was going to get me back home," she said. "I never was afraid."

The journey from San Francisco to Pearl Harbor could have tested a lesser faith. The Pacific was extremely rough, with high seas and horrible weather. Of the seventy-five women on the ship, only ten were able to walk off under their own power when they arrived at Pearl Harbor. The rest had to be carried off, too weak from seasickness to move. Winnie was used to the ocean and was not frightened. Instead, she spent the voyage giving soda crackers and ginger ale to the seasick WAVES.

At Pearl Harbor, Winnie became an aviation machinist. Her job was to help strip down planes that had been damaged during battle before they would be repaired or junked. Sometimes, the cockpits would be bloody or gory from a pilot who had been wounded or killed in action, but Winnie and the other WAVES did their job.

Winnie also had time to explore Hawaii, riding in a convertible to a roast on the Nuuanu Pali Lookout on Oahu or watching the farmers burn the tops of the pineapple trees. "It was beautiful," she said. And she ate pineapple three times a day. "I still like pineapple," she said.

In January 1946, Winnie, then a seaman first class, was discharged from the WAVES and headed home. "I'd have stayed in if they kept women, but they were going to disband the WAVES," she said.

While away from Maine, Winnie had written to her mother every week. Her mother wrote to all three children in the service every week. After a friend of Winnie's had read her mother's letters and asked if she might write him, her mother wrote him too for the rest of the war and for several years after. Wanting to surprise her parents, Winnie did not tell them that she was coming home. Instead, she wrote a stack of letters and left them with a friend to mail one each day. It took her five days to reach Lincoln, much to her parents' surprise and delight. The last letter arrived the day after she did.

With the war behind her (her brother and sister had returned from the service before she did), Winnie dedicated herself to giving back to her family and community. On November 23, 1946, she married her high school boyfriend, Alfred Clemons, who had served in the Army and fought in the Battle of the Bulge. Winnie and Alfred had two children: Anna and Glenn. Together, they worked the family potato farm in Lee and attended St. Mary's Church in Lincoln. They instilled in their children a sense of service and the need to give back. Their daughter, Anna, became a nurse; and their son, Glenn, enlisted in the Army, as Alfred had. Winnie's grandson, Blaine, enlisted in the Navy in honor of his grandmother's service. He now lives in Alaska and works for the supplemental insurance company AFLAC.

Sadly, Alfred, Anna and Glenn have all passed away, but Winnie, now ninety, remains active and dedicated to giving back before receiving. Winnie belongs to the Veterans of Foreign Wars, the American Legion, and the Legion Auxiliary. She volunteers at St. Mary's Church and at a nursing home, and, until recently, sang in a group.

The great "adventure" of serving in the WAVES opened her eyes to the fact that "the world was a large, large place."

"It's made me a better person," she said. "I think I appreciated lots of things I wouldn't have if I'd stayed here."

Recently, Winnie received a State of Maine Silver Commemorative Coin in honor of her service. The coin has the likeness of the Women Veterans Plaque that hangs in the Hall of Flags at the State House in Augusta.

Winnie acknowledged that she has received much in her life: a loving, close-knit family, a friendly and supportive hometown, and as much adventure as she could ever have hoped for. "I'm truly blessed," she said. But she has never stopped giving.

"I'd do it all again if I could," she said of her military service. That sentiment applied just as well to raising a family, working the farm, and living in Maine. "I have tried to live every day to the fullest, and I have."

14

JOHN LEE

Everybody's His Own Boss and Everybody's a Little Bit Different

John Lee (born 1920) has always been his own boss, with an eye for a little mischief and an ability to hold his own, no matter the situation. As a child, John used to steal cigarette butts from his father's ashtray then race to the King's Chair, a giant elm on the corner of Atlantic and Monument streets in Portland, where he'd smoke the butts out of reach of any adult. Whether dodging older kids while he dog-paddled off the East End Beach or learning how to drive the "nuns' bus" in the West End from his father, John, the second youngest of five children, was ready to grow up.

John got his chance one summer night in 1939 while working at the Greyhound bus garage in Portland's West End. John had graduated from high school the year before and, after several months working in the garage, wanted to get out and do something different.

"That's where I met a man who was in the National Guard, name of Emery," John said. "He was a captain in the National Guard. He used to park his car there. Some nights, he'd come in, probably 9 o'clock at night and it was pretty quiet and we'd shoot the bull. I got to know him pretty well."

After quitting the garage, John received a call from Emery. "He wanted to pick me up, take me down to the armory. Look the outfits over. I said okay. I went down and I was thinking about it anyhow, even before that, joining the guard. Anyhow, I joined up that night."

Once John joined, his friend, Emery, quickly defined their new relationship. "I played pool with some guys. Emery came out. *Captain* Emery came," John corrected himself, emphasizing the man's rank. "And he started talking to me. He said: 'Oh, by the way, when I'm in uniform, you say 'sir.' So, anyhow, I did say sir from then on."

While stationed with the Army National Guard on Cushing's Island in Casco Bay, John heard the news of the Japanese attack on Pearl Harbor.

"I was up in the 12-inch guns," he said. "My girlfriend was with me, who ended up being my wife. It was a Sunday. They alerted everybody because they didn't know what the hell was going on. Nobody did. So we had to go up in the guns and the people visiting us had to stay down in the barracks. We stayed up there for two, three hours, I guess. Quite a while, then they called us back down. We had live ammunition. We had powder. Everything was manned. Ready to go. Just needed a target."

John got his target eventually, as he was called up to fight and shipped over to England. At the replacement depot in England, "you can bounce around like a ping pong ball." John was in England for some time, training on automatic weapons, like the 40mm cannon and .50s machine guns on half-tracks. His unit was always on the move, from Land's End to Dover, usually stationed around fighter bases.

"I was a junior lieutenant. I led the convoys," John explained. "The senior lieutenant would have to go out ahead. They'd get through and get all this information for the particular area they were going to defend. The senior platoon leader would have to go to that point and pick out gun positions. Four gun positions for four 40 mm guns and usually we'd pack one half-track with each gun. Then I'd come along with the outfit. Each gun would drop off to a man. Gun 1 would drop off to a man. Gun 2 to another one. Three to another one. Four to another one. They'd take those guns and set them up. We didn't get any warnings about any moves. All of a sudden, the telephone would ring: 'Hey, get down to Land's End as quick as you can.' Land's End might be 100 miles away, or up to Dover."

While stationed in England, John got his first experience with the German V-1 rockets.

"One night, right after D-Day, we got this roaring, throbbing in the air," John said. "All you could see was a flame flying. We didn't know what the hell was going on. It was a bomb, the V-1. Nobody knew anything about them. We were shooting at those. But most of the guns were shooting at the flame. That's behind it. I don't know why they didn't flip it ahead of the flame. We didn't hit any that night. They had them in the daytime, too, going for London. Then they started hitting them, knocking a few down. Get them in the air and they'd explode. It was a hell of an explosion."

Finally, six or seven days after D-Day, John got his orders to ship to France with his unit, the 635th Automatic Weapons Battalion. They landed on Omaha Beach, which had just been secured and was humming with activity.

"There was an awful lot of supplies on [Omaha Beach]," he said. "Quite a few men on it. Working supplies, I guess, gasoline, ammunition, stuff like that.

"We landed there," John said. "We set up for one night. I know everybody was a little bit skittish because you had gunfire off in the distance. All of a sudden, you had one that sounded like it was over your head. We'd never been in combat before."

Then they moved off the beach.

"We were positioned just off the beach and that was an experience, believe me," John said. "None of us had been in combat before, see. You wondered where are [the Germans]? Not a light anywhere. You had a map of roads and a flashlight. And you'd duck down under the hood or the dashboard to look at it. Well, anyhow, that's how we traveled off the beach."

They left Omaha at night, which was harrowing.

"I didn't like it myself," John said. "It was pitch black. No lights. They did have a couple of MP's close to the beach at intersections. They wouldn't even flash a light until someone was coming on the road. Then they might flash it once and stop the vehicle to see what it was all about. That's all. Believe me, you'd be thinking all night long, what's going on here, where are they now? You'd expect to see someone jump out of the brush there anytime."

The tall hedgerows also made it impossible to know what was just up ahead or around the bend.

"The roads [had] hedges on each side," John said. "Believe me, they were thick and they were tall. They were probably average six feet tall, the hedge itself. Then they had those bushes in front of it. And they'd have these little holes in it where the infantry had come through; just crawl through. It was an experience."

One of the biggest problems was that soldiers constantly got lost. "During our conferences, before we moved, we'd have what's called the lost vehicle rendezvous point," John said. "You'd have a point, if there was a church—in a small town, the church. There was always a church in a small town. If they got lost, go there and wait. Then it was my job to find them. I'd just go to that point, that church, and nine out of ten times, they were there waiting for me. They were awfully glad to see me that [first] night because they were kicking around in the rubble and found some things that kind of woke them up a little bit. They found a few bodies. The battle had just gone through there. They hadn't had time to really clean up the area. German bodies."

As his platoon moved across Normandy, it bounced from division to division, wherever it was needed. "We were always moving some place," John said. "We'd move across divisional lines. You might call it a rebel outfit. We'd get the orders to go to here and it might be another Army area. We didn't know."

His platoon typically defended important installations like airports, bridges and roads from enemy airplanes, or engaged in infantry support, but rarely found themselves in close fire.

"Once you get so you could fire the damn things, you didn't even think about it," he said. "You just shoot it. It's not like I'm shooting at you, I can see you. It's not like that. You don't know who's up there in a plane. Those were our targets. A couple of times they used our half-tracks to kill the infantry. We'd empty the guns, then we'd move the half-track, maybe fifty yards, just in case they lobbed a couple mortars over. We never lost a half-track, but we took precautions. Did get some mortars a couple times, but never lost a half-track."

After fighting near towns from Carentan to Avranches, where they defended a bridge against Luftwaffe attacks for several weeks, John's unit headed to Paris, "but the Germans bailed out of Paris before we got to it, so we bypassed Paris. And we came right up into Belgium. Luxembourg. Bastogne." Along the way, they met many civilians and found small slices of normalcy where they could, like attending mass.

"When we first got there, I don't remember the name of the place, but it was to the west of Bastogne," John said. "Bastogne hadn't been hurt then. It was a nice town, small town. Square with a fountain in it. We were bivouacked to the west. The front lines were ahead of us. We didn't know where. I went to church that Sunday. There was a priest. A big house. Tremendous house. There was one room there where they had several civilians and maybe a dozen dogfaces, GI's, for Sunday mass. They passed the collection plate. Nobody had any dough, so, if you had them, you tossed in a pack of cigarettes. Cigarettes were worth money, if you wanted to sell them. So, anyhow, that's what we did. I didn't have any money. I had a cigarette ration coming."

While they were in France, John and his platoon would often trade their K-rations and Cracker Jack boxes with locals for eggs or, maybe, a chicken. One time, John and Sergeant Morgan, from his platoon, "were out hitting some farms in France. We got some eggs. There was a chicken running around the yard. Now, Morgan could talk German and most of those people, I think, understood German, because he'd talk German to them and they'd understand. We bartered for a chicken."

But trading for the chicken was only the beginning. Then they had to catch the chicken, which proved very elusive. "Finally, we tried to hit it with our army carbine," he said. "You ever try shooting a chicken with an army carbine? I think we ran out of ammunition before we got the goddamned chicken. We were trying to hit it in the neck. When it stopped, we fired."

By the time they left Bastogne and headed to St. Vith, in Belgium, it was almost Christmas, and the Nazis had begun their largest counterattack.

"All of a sudden, trucks are going by with men in it," John recalled. "No guns. The guys are hollering out: 'Better get out of there. They're not too far behind us.' They were running. They left their guns. They didn't have a chance to get them."

John had never participated in a retreat before, but as a second lieutenant in charge of his platoon, he found himself giving orders.

"The word came out, burn all the gasoline unless you can take it out," John said. "There was a pile of gasoline in five gallon cans. There was one pile, a lot of gasoline and nobody was there. I told them to burn that gasoline. So he hit it and set it on fire with his quad-50. Then we bailed out. We were heading back to Bastogne. We were on a country road, then came into a main road. It was well-traveled. There was a lot of traffic on it. We were just getting on it and word came out there were a couple tanks coming up the road. We had guns that would take care of light tanks, not the heavies. We pulled out the guns but didn't dig pits." The guns were usually anchored in pits.

There was a big farmhouse and a ditch beside the road. One of the gun sections set up by the farmhouse, pointing toward a large hill, where it expected the Nazi tanks to appear. Just as John arrived to check on that gun section, the tanks appeared behind them, from the other direction.

"One hit above us, down 50 yards from us," John recalled. "I went down around this farmhouse. There was a courtyard there. While I'm starting to go around, this guy on the tank is blazing away with machine guns and everything else. I dove into a pile of horse manure. Dove right into it. When that cannon hit, that's when we knew that the tanks were down behind us. I got out of that pile of horse manure and got behind a brick wall in the courtyard."

Two Nazi tanks and jeeps were approximately five hundred yards away and had John and his men pinned down.

"So we got the hell out of there," John said. They lost a half dozen men, including one of Tom's radio operators, who was killed by a shell. As John's unit headed south from Bastogne to a large supply depot, they passed the 101st Airborne, who would play a pivotal role in the American victory in the Battle of the Bulge.

"Then things started to open up a little bit," John said. "Germany really shot their wad right there [in the Battle of the Bulge]. Our next move was out to the Rhine River. On top of the cliffs lining the river were machine gun holes with men living up there. And it was solid rock. So they took a bunch of 40 mm guns and lined them up. Those shells on the 40 mm will only go so far and then self-destruct. Those were just within that cone of fire. That night, the infantry jumped off and crossed the river. They got across all right. We lost a few guys, not too many. The engineers down below put a pontoon bridge across, so the next day, we went across. We holed up there for a couple days."

It was a frigid winter, but "we had clothes for cold weather," he said. "We were all right. Infantry people, like the airborne, they had what they had on their back. That was it. One pair of shoes in that kind of weather, your feet are going to get wet all the time. They had a lot of problems, freezing their feet. We didn't have any of that. We lived a different way. We were more comfortable, put it that way. We could get warm."

After crossing the Rhine, John and his division headed across Germany. At one bridge, they found a device the Germans had left.

"It had rockets in it," John said. "I guess a dozen. Just a little armored place for a man to be. He could pull a lever and touch them off. We all went over to see it, but didn't fool around with it." John's platoon left, but the supply sergeant stayed behind. "All of a sudden, there was a whooshing sound. A big cloud of dust come over there where that was. All of a sudden, there was arms and legs coming out of that cloud of dust. The supply sergeant. He'd touched them off. Scared the living hell out of him. They all burst in the sky. But it was funny as hell to see him come out of that cloud."

John's platoon had almost reached Dresden when Germany surrendered on May 7. "We stopped shooting," John said. "The war's all over. The next morning, a couple of German planes were flying over. The pilot was waving at us. We couldn't shoot at him. If we could, it would've knocked him out of the sky. That's for damn sure." Instead, John waved back.

After returning home in 1945, John finally got to spend some time with his wife, Rose Woods, whom he had married before shipping out. "I'd only been with her a couple weeks before I was gone for two years," he said. They had met while roller-skating at the Elm Street Rink in Portland. "She was a good skater," John recalled. "She had her own skates."

The next step was to get a job, and John wasted no time. "I really didn't have a job before I left, fresh out of high school," he said, so he asked his sister, who was a supervisor at the telephone company, if she could find a job for him. She did, as a cable-splicer. "Monday morning, I went to work for the telephone company. I didn't take any time off. I didn't even have a place to live. I had to live with my folks, me and my wife, three or four weeks, until I found a place to live."

Except for his service during the Korean War, John would stay with the telephone company until he retired.

"I liked to work. [Cable-splicing] wasn't monotonous. It wasn't the same thing every day. It was a good-paying job at the time. Then I went on the test board when I got older. The test board is the telephone office where you test lines, troubleshoot. Sitting at the goddamned test board was like sitting at a desk for me. I was used to being outside, my own boss, so to speak, all day long, except when my own boss came around to check on me." John worked as a cable-splicer for twenty years, then on the test board for over a dozen years before retiring.

John and Rose also quickly started a family. By the time he was called up for the Korean War in 1951, they had three children under the age of five: Greg, Rebecca and Sandra. Their fourth, Joanne, was born after he returned from Korea.

Because he had served as "Head Communications Officer" in the National Guard after World War II, the Army assigned him to be the communications officer for the 10th Corps Artillery. Before traveling to Korea, he stopped in Japan to study how to protect oneself from the effects of the atomic bombs.

"I did see Nagasaki," he said. "Oh, Jesus, not a hell of a lot left."

The eight months he spent in Korea "[c]ould've been a lot tougher; could've been a lot worse," he said. "They were still fighting, but they were more or less stagnant." John did visit a front-line outpost. "You could see the enemy line from there. It was pretty quiet, so I didn't mind that.

"I always thought military life was a pretty good life, if you keep your nose clean," he said. "I'd recommend it to anybody."

What John remembers most fondly about his military service and his work for the telephone company is the opportunity to meet lots of different people and to be his own boss.

"Everybody's his own boss; how he acts and so forth," John said. "Everybody's a little bit different."

15

HENRY WOZNIAK

Do the Right Thing at the Right Time

Over almost three years of service on the USS *North Carolina*, including immediately after Pearl Harbor, when it was the only battleship in the Pacific, Henry Wozniak learned a valuable lesson that he carried with him the rest of his life: do the right thing at the right time. He also learned a second lesson: "Get to be an officer. The food is better. The pay is better. The clothes is better."

Henry grew up in Farmington, Connecticut, and then joined the Civilian Conservation Corps, working as a storekeeper in Connecticut. He handed out rakes, shovels, picks and machetes, and was in charge of the dynamite. "It was an easy job," he said. "I sat in the window all day and read books."

But Henry wanted more excitement, so he joined the Navy in early 1941. Before the war, Henry was stationed in Casco Bay. At night, he could hear the snorkel sounds of German subs recharging their batteries. Henry would signal to anti-sub boats that there was a sub in harbor. One night, at 2 a.m., he heard depth charges and could hear them cheer that they got a sub.

Henry was then assigned to the battleship USS *North Carolina*, which was commissioned on April 9, 1941, and was the first of ten fast battleships to join the American fleet in World War II. The *North Carolina* fought in every major naval battle in the Pacific theater, earning fifteen battle stars. It was the most highly decorated battleship in World War II. The *North Carolina* was the first new battleship to arrive in the Pacific since the start of the war.

Henry served on the battleship for thirty-three months as an electrician in turret two. His primary job was to test for resistance for the primers on the sixteen-inch guns. To shoot one sixteen-inch shell required 600 pounds of powder. A shell for bombardment weighs 1500. An armor-piercing shell weighs 2700 pounds.

During his nearly three years, Henry saw a tremendous amount of combat, working constantly to make sure the 16-inch guns operated as needed. During one battle, a five-inch gun exploded near him. "Knocked me on my ass," he said. "I came to in sick bay three days later." Henry lost a good amount of his hearing as a result of that explosion and now has only 12 percent of it.

Henry and the *North Carolina* first helped the Marines land on Guadalcanal and then guarded the supply and communication lines in the Solomon Islands, engaging in the Battle of the Eastern Solomons, helping save the carrier *Enterprise*. The *North Carolina* fought in the months-long Battle of Guadalcanal and was torpedoed, but was quickly patched up. From Guam to the Mariana Islands, from New Guinea to the Marshall Islands, and many, many more, the number of operations the *North Carolina* participated in are almost too many to name.

The *North Carolina* typically carried 900 shells on board. During the bombing of New Guinea, Henry recalls expending eight times that number. The supply ship bringing them ammunition from nearby New Caledonia blew up. "It was the biggest explosion I ever saw in my life," Henry said, because it was carrying tons and tons of powder bags to supply eleven battleships.

When the *North Carolina* bombarded Saipan harbor, Henry could see people jumping off cliffs. Apparently, the Japanese citizens had been told that the Americans would torture them if they caught them. "I could see it," Henry said." We were three-quarters of a mile away. With binoculars, we could see the color of their eyes."

Off the west coast of Japan, they recovered several American pilots who had been shot down. During the Battle of the Philippines, the *North Carolina* fought off its first kamikaze attack. Despite all its battles, the *North Carolina* lost only ten men and had sixty-seven wounded in the entire war.

When the battleship returned to Pearl Harbor for overhaul, Henry received word that his mother had suffered a heart attack. The chaplain called him and said: "you have more time than anyone else on the ship. I'm going to relieve you. I'm going to send you back. Have your bag packed." Said Henry: "That was the end of my war."

While stationed in San Diego, Henry married his wife, Lillian. After being discharged, Henry and Lillian moved to Long Beach, Long Island, and ran an electrical company for five years. He then started an ice cream business, called "Mr. Softie," which distributed ice cream products in Connecticut, Massachusetts and Rhode Island. Henry then ran a tool company for twenty-eight years, retiring in 1988 to his camp in Rangeley. Lillian passed away on March 27, 2007, but he still has three grown children, eleven grandchildren and eleven great-grandchildren.

And Henry has told them all: "Try to get an education; the best that you possibly could." If you join the military, "stay out of the trenches. Get to be an officer. The food is better. The pay is better. The clothes is better." But, most importantly, "Do the right thing at the right time." It is what got him and the *North Carolina* home safely.

16

PHIL CURRAN

Choose Your Friends Carefully

On December 7, 1941, Phil Curran, who lived on Peak's Island with his parents and three siblings, had agreed to accompany a shy friend, whose courage needed boosting, on a date with his girlfriend. As they munched brownies and listened to the symphony on the radio, a bulletin interrupted with news of the attack.

"We were absolutely shattered," Phil recalled.

Life for Phil before Pearl Harbor had been full of fishing and swimming on the islands. Phil's mother was from Orr's Island, where the family had been located until they moved to Peak's. Phil's father worked for Casco Bay Lines.

The day after Pearl Harbor, at 10 a.m., Portland High School held an assembly to discuss the attack. "On that day, about ten seniors joined the service right then and there. We had a really passionate hour or so. Teachers were talking with us and trying to calm us down."

But Phil, a freshman, was too young to enlist right away. Two years later, at age seventeen, on May 1, 1944, he enlisted despite having one year left of high school. "We couldn't wait. It was such an intense period of patriotism. We've never seen it since and I don't know if they'd ever seen it before. I was a junior when I turned seventeen. I just jumped out of school and went into the Navy as soon as I could do it. It was such an intense kind of passion in the country amongst all of us that my parents agreed to this. They weren't the only ones because the service was full of young people."

As he left to enlist, Phil met his father at the Casco Bay Lines office. During a tearful goodbye, Phil's father gave some advice that he was to repeat frequently in letters to his son: "Don't drink. Choose your friends carefully. Don't do anything you wouldn't want your mother to know about."

Phil recalled boot camp as fast-paced and designed to get sailors into service as quickly as possible. "Everybody had to go to recruit training. They call it boot camp. Nowadays, and before that war, and ever since, the recruit training is usually three months. During the war, everything was accelerated, including recruit training. My recruit training was five weeks. During that period, somebody somewhere decided what your career in the Navy was going to be like. I assume they took that from the [aptitude] tests. I got my orders and my orders were to radio school. That had been accelerated to a five-and-a-half month course, rather than its original eighteen months because they had to feed the fleet."

The Navy sent Phil to radio school in Samson, New York, where he took a range of radio-related courses, including Morse Code. "In order to graduate from Navy radio school, you had a minimum of handling eighteen words a minute, Morse Code," Phil said. "That's pretty brisk. Before I got through, when I got into the fleet and was really tight with it, I got up to a speed of thirty-eight words per minute."

Phil graduated from radio school on November 27, 1944. "We were all scared together. Absolutely, totally scared to death. There was a lot of action going on. The word was out that our class was going to be assigned in the South Pacific to the amphibious corps. They go up on the beaches. And they have to have a radio man. So we were all committed mentally to going into the amphibs and going into the South Pacific and being shot at. And that's what happened. My whole class went into the amphibs. Don't ask me how this happened, but I went onto an admiral's staff who was a commander of a huge amphibious force."

In December, the Navy assigned Phil to the radio staff of Vice-Admiral Daniel E. Barbey, commander of the Seventh Fleet's amphibious force located in the South Pacific.

"I spent the rest of my time in the Navy with him."

But first Phil had to get to the South Pacific.

"The Navy's policy, they had a classification of transportation where you paid your own way if you could. If you couldn't, they'd take care of it and get you there. The kicker was this: If you paid your own way, you could take ten days to get there. If they paid your way, you left immediately."

Phil found his brother, who was at quartermaster school, and asked him to send a message home to their mother, asking for the transportation money. After a ten-day leave back in Maine, Phil bought his train ticket to the receiving station in San Jose, California. From there, he traveled by Army transport to Subec Bay.

But he couldn't find the fleet.

"It took a long time to catch up because they couldn't find [Barbey]," Phil said. "He was moving too fast. I'd get to one spot and he'd be gone. I was assigned to an army transport ship to go into the South Pacific and catch up with the command. I got as far as the Admiralty Islands where he was supposed to be at the time. He was gone. So I jumped another Army ship and got another ride to Finschafen, New Guinea, where he had just finished up an operation and he wasn't there.

"I remember thinking, how are they going to win this war without me?" Phil asked, laughing.

Phil finally caught up with Barbey on Easter morning and immediately went on an operation near Borneo.

The USS *Blue Ridge* was the first flagship on which Phil served. Admirals and above are flag officers. When an admiral is based on a ship, that ship flies the admiral's pennant, or flag. Flagships, Phil recalled, were "not very impressive ships. They're not battleships. They were designed early in the war to be specifically command ships."

While learning his way around the ship, Phil immediately went to work in the large radio room. About a dozen radio operators would be on a shift at one time, and the radio room was always busy.

"We had a lot of traffic. Every ship in the force had to report to the admiral."

Phil and the other radio operators would receive and send messages. One-way communications that just had to be typed down were easier. Ship-to-ship communications required more skill. Radio operators had to remember five characters at once.

"The communications never stopped," Phil said.

The force participated in twelve operations in the South Pacific, but, thankfully, "much of the stuff I saw was from a distance." However, he was on the front line during his entire service. "All the time that I was assigned to the admiral . . . I was in a combat area." Phil recalled being issued knives and gas masks. "Everybody knew we were going to invade Japan. We knew that we were right in the front line for that."

But the war ended, and then began what Phil called his truly "valuable duty."

On August 15, while peace was being negotiated, Admiral Barbey and his staff on the USS *Catoctin*, including Phil, were ordered to prepare to land occupation forces in Korea. On their way from Manila to Okinawa to pick up Marines, they had to fight through a typhoon "that bounced up all over the channels south of Formosa for four days."

Barbey and his staff arrived at Jinsen (now Incheon), Korea, on September 8. The next day, the Japanese emperor surrendered all his country's ground and air forces in Korea south of the 38th parallel to Admiral Barbey's group of officers, led by General Hodge and Admiral Kinkaid.

"Why, it was so exciting," Phil said. "As soon as the Japanese surrendered, the Chinese started jockeying [the Chinese Civil War]. We were right in the middle of that. The admiral was right in the middle of it because it was interfering with his mission. That was very exciting stuff." Phil even witnessed fighting between Chinese nationalists and communists.

"We headed for the coast of China following the surrender of Japanese forces in Korea," Phil said, "to make a series of occupational landings over the next three months, engage in the negotiations of surrendering units, establish the U.S. positions with each of the rival communist factions, much of it confrontational, and supervise landings of the Chinese Nationalist Army."

Phil spent three months in the Yellow Sea. His final port-of-call was Shanghai. On Thanksgiving Day, he headed for home. Phil was discharged from the Navy on May 30, 1946, after twenty-five months of service.

"Most of it had been exciting and eventful for an island boy, even then only nineteen years old," Phil wrote, later in life. "Nevertheless, I shall always call that day the happiest day of my life. We were at peace. I was home. I hitchhiked from Bosto,n where I had been discharged, and was let off by my benefactor in Portland on the most beautiful and sparkling sunny day of the year."

When he arrived home, his mother asked him what he ate for breakfast in the Navy. "Steak and eggs," he lied, and that is what he got.

"The first thing I did when I got out of the Navy was to go back to school," he said. Just a junior when he enlisted, Phil returned to finish his senior year and graduate from Portland High School. Anxious to pursue his education, Phil attended Portland Junior College (now part of the University of Southern Maine) on the G.I. Bill. But then the Korean War erupted.

Phil did not hesitate to enlist again.

"I thought it was the thing to do," he said. "I was trained."

Because of his radio skills, the Navy sent him to Radio Washington, part of the Navy's radio system. Not much had changed. Radio operators were still using the same hand-keys and teletype, so Phil did not need any retraining.

Phil spent two years in Washington, D.C., and enjoyed his time there. "It really was an experience for a radio guy like me to be in Washington. It was a real treat. It was like going to graduate school."

But, "that wasn't what I left home for."

One night, while Phil was on watch with his chief, he was complaining that he had enlisted so he could serve in Korea, not in Washington. After his chief told him to tell Main Radio that he "wanted to get on a ship and go to sea," Phil did exactly that.

"They were tickled to death to see me at Main Navy," he said. "They were building a ship in Boston, which was just right up my alley. I talked with the captain of the ship's staffing detail. He said 'you're just the man I want.' Before I knew it, I was on my way to Boston. Before I knew it, we were out doing sea trials."

Phil sailed on the USS *Salem*, a heavy cruiser, which is a class between battleship and cruiser.

"I just loved that ship. I had to wait awhile for her to be commissioned. I was on the commissioning detail. Then you have to go on sea trials and have to test everything, including the radio. We were in the Atlantic Fleet, but in the Caribbean quite a lot. The Panama Canal. We went into the Mediterranean."

Phil served on command ships for assault carriers, but his service in the Korean War was quieter than during World War II. "The Navy didn't have the same role there that it did during the Second World War," he said.

Phil saw even more of the world during the Korean War than he had during World War II. The Caribbean. The northern coast of Africa. Phil spent five months in the Mediterranean Sea, operating out of Villa France, near Monte Carlo. "I liked the southern beaches in France," he said. "We had a lot of nice times."

Phil enjoyed sailing around the world, and his Maine roots helped him handle the open seas. During World War II and the Korean War, "the Navy took me to twenty-eight different countries and I never got seasick." When some sailors could not stand radio watch because they were too seasick and had to sleep in a lifeboat on deck, he would cover their watch.

After the Korean War, Phil graduated from the School of Banking at Williams College and entered the banking business, going to work for Casco Bank and Trust, where he worked for thirty-nine years. Phil and his wife, Nancy, were married in 1965, and live on a farm that has been in his wife's family since 1775. "We proudly and intentionally still hold almost half [of the original 100 acres]." Phil and Nancy have raised four children (Colleen, Dennis, Martha and Andrew) and have seven grandchildren and five great-grandchildren.

Phil has used his radio skills only once since his service ended. While he and Nancy were living in Brunswick, they made friends with some of the pilots stationed at the Brunswick Naval Air Station. One Sunday morning, a pilot invited him to come with him on base. "I said, oh yes, sure," he said. "I'll be darned but they had a radio shack. I think it was like twelve years since I'd touched a key." He asked if he could use the radio. "I started belting that," he recalled. "I had learned to be a high-speed operator. I started playing with that key and I surprised myself. Pretty soon, all these people are coming around and listening to it. It was music to my soul. I haven't done it since."

While Phil has not used his radio skills in decades, he has continued to serve his country and his community in countless ways, including as president of the Westbrook City Council, a member of the Maine House of Representatives, president of the Portland Metro and of the Westbrook Community Hospital, as a board member for the Maine School for the Blind, Goodwill Industries and Prides Training School (for people with special needs), and as a board president and backup preacher for the

Maine Conference of the United Church of Christ. Phil and Nancy also helped found the Maine Irish Children's Program, traveling to Belfast, Northern Ireland, in 1985 to arrange for ten- to twelve-year-old children to spend their summers in Maine.

And Phil has spent a lifetime following his father's advice to choose his friends carefully.

"I went into the Navy so young that I was learning things in the Navy that I normally would have been learning from my dad," Phil recalled. "So there's a lot of the learning process I left home without. My father was a very easygoing, gentle man. I don't know how many letters he wrote to me and he always ended it the same way: 'Choose your friends carefully and don't drink.' I still tell my children the same thing no matter where they go: 'Choose your friends carefully.'"

Phil remains in touch with friends he made while in the Navy, and their wives have also become friends. "We got caught up in the ship's reunions and our wives understood what good people we were taking up with, that they thought were all idiots when they married us," he said, with a laugh. "We've mentioned this more than once: what good friends we made out of that group of Navy people and Navy wives."

Phil's daughter, Martha, is also a Navy wife. Her husband, Raymond Goyet from Brown Street in Westbrook, is a captain in the Navy. "That's no small stuff," Phil said. "I have been very, very, very pleased and have let her know it, that my daughter has been such a good Navy wife." Other people "don't really know what the Navy is like except for what they see in the movies. It's not like that at all."

Phil and his family experienced the tragic part of military service on June 28, 2011, when Martha's son, Marine Corporal Mark

Goyet, was killed in Afghanistan's Helmand Province. Mark was assigned to the 3rd Battalion, 4th Marine Regiment, 1st Marine Division, I Marine Expeditionary Force out of Twentynine Palms, California. He had already received the Purple Heart, Combat Action Ribbon, National Defense Service Medal, Global War on Terrorism Service Medal, Marine Corps Good Conduct Medal, and the Afghanistan Campaign Medal.

"He was a very popular guy, a very thoughtful guy," Phil said. "He was the kind of guy who would take people under his wing."

Like his grandfather, Mark chose his friends wisely, and once he had, he was dedicated to them, even volunteering to return to Afghanistan. "Mark didn't have to go," said his father in a newspaper interview shortly after his son's death. "All he had to do was bide his time, but Mark had a sense of commitment to friends he grew up with who didn't make it back or were badly injured in Afghanistan."

One year later, on Memorial Day in Westbrook's Riverbank Park, Phil spoke of his grandson's service to his country and to his friends, whom he had chosen wisely and served faithfully.

17

LORING HART

Education Provides Opportunities

While Loring Hart put his education at Bowdoin College on hold to serve in General Patton's Third Army, his college experience gave him opportunities few other soldiers had, including teaching in Germany and attending school in France. Once the war was over, the G.I. Bill gave him the opportunity to finish his degree at Bowdoin, earn a master's degree from the University of Miami and a PhD from Harvard University. That experience gave him the opportunity to spend the rest of his life in education, ultimately serving as president for two different colleges.

School was an important part of Loring's early life. The Bath native was the valedictorian of his high school class in 1942 and enrolled at nearby Bowdoin College. But then the war came calling and Loring answered, enlisting in the Army after one semester at Bowdoin. After spending a few days being processed at Fort Devens, Massachusetts, Loring was sent to Camp Blanding, Florida, for basic training in the infantry. He spent seventeen weeks learning how to shoot a rifle and accept orders "unquestioningly," as well as getting into top physical shape, culminating with a 30-mile march at night in the countryside.

After a brief visit home, where he received "all kinds of support" from his parents, friends and girlfriend, he reported to Camp Kilmer, New Jersey. From there, he would find out if he were going to Europe or to the Pacific. "Nobody wanted to go to the Pacific," Loring said. The Pacific was hot, farther away from home, and more unfamiliar than Europe. And, many troops were afraid of the Japanese troops because of the "feeling that the Japanese were totally uncivilized."

Loring got the assignment he was hoping for and shipped out to Europe in the fall of 1943. "I can remember walking up the gangplank, with either the officer or a noncom standing to the right with a list of names," he said. As the names were called and the soldiers sounded off in reply, "[y]ou were on your way to Europe."

Loring was assigned a bunk on the lowest deck (G deck, with A deck being the top deck), well below the water line and "hot as the devil," but he quickly found a cooler spot on the A deck. And he was fortunate to be traveling across the Atlantic on a converted luxury liner instead of a smaller transport ship, which could be tossed about by the rough ocean waves. "Seasickness was no joke," he said, but the large ship made passage much easier.

He made it to Scotland safely, with no U-boat sightings and took a train to Edinburgh, Scotland, then to Honiton, England, which, the future professor of English literature was quick to point out, was one of the settings for Jane Austen's *Sense and Sensibility*. This was August 1944, two months after D-Day, and "[t]hey were waiting to find room for us to go to Europe."

They quickly found room for him in General Patton's 3rd Army, 4th Armored Division, and ferried him across the English Channel to Normandy, where he landed on Omaha Beach. "I can remember you were taken across the channel," he said. "And you were taken ashore and there were the cliffs that you see in all the films and movies and so on, and you walked up a path that went up the cliffs. And as you went up the cliffs, you'd see a line on your right, going down them. The boys going down them had on grey uniforms. They were [captured] Germans. They were on their way to the United States of America and some of them in the woods right here in Maine [at prisoner camps]. So you looked at these guys; they were going to America and where were you going?" Private Loring Hart was on his way to Germany.

Loring was a radio operator on a half-track truck, moving across France. By September 1944, the front had moved "considerably" and he met up with it in Alsace-Lorraine, a "no man's land between France and Germany and it's been overrun for centuries either by the French or the Germans."

It rained constantly in Alsace-Lorraine, but there was no fighting close by. Patton soon received orders to break through the German lines, with the 4th Armored Division out front. "We went north out of Alsace-Lorraine before turning to the east. By that time, the 101st Airborne had been overrun," Loring said. "And the Germans were holding Bastogne [Belgium]. And the 4th Armored Division got the orders to break through it and to relieve Bastogne. Open it up."

As the 4th Armored Division approached Bastogne through the surrounding countryside, American soldiers would pop out of their foxholes to ask if they had any "ten-in-ones," which were the Army's latest version of rations.

"The Army was constantly trying to improve rations," Loring said. "First came C-rations, which came in cans and were practically inedible. Unappetizing. Then they moved into K-rations, which were much better and sophisticated; came in cardboard boxes with candy and treats in them. The next move was to ten-in-one rations, which came in very large packages and were full of lots of goodies. So these guys in the foxholes were very interested in them."

Loring's division entered Bastogne at night and occupied several buildings that had been damaged by bombing, but were still standing. Relieved to be out of the rain, the soldiers grabbed bedding on the second floor.

"That lasted a couple of nights until the Germans pulled an air raid on Bastogne," he said. "You ever seen people go down a flight of stairs in one step? The Germans came over at night and really unloaded on Bastogne. And the idea was, really, to get down those stairs, man, and into the cellar.

"All you thought about was your immediate safety and doing something about it and getting out of there," he continued. "Your basic instincts took over."

A major in the division later told Loring that "of all the experiences that all of us went through, he was most frightened that night. He didn't think we'd make it."

After huddling in the basement all night, the men were ordered out of the building and into foxholes. It was winter and the ground was frozen. "If you're going to dig a foxhole, you have to get through the frost," Loring said. "You have to chop your way and get below the surface of the earth, so you can stretch out. That takes some digging."

The shelling continued for several days until the division was ordered to pull back. Despite the heavy shelling, Bastogne had been secured, and the 4th Armored Division was on its way to Germany with Patton. As the Americans crossed the Rhine River into Germany on a pontoon bridge, Patton urinated into the river to show his contempt for the Germans.

All these years later, Loring worried that he was not conveying how difficult and dangerous it was to move through these areas. Traveling from France to Belgium and to Germany "sounds like a field trip on a holiday," he said. "It wasn't." There was constant German resistance. "You were trying to keep alive and make sure the Germans didn't." But, he acknowledged, "[t]he human mind has a tendency to close out unpleasant episodes. I think I've probably forgotten a number of unpleasant episodes that have been erased over the years."

From Germany, Patton's 3rd Army, including the 4th Armored Division, was ordered into Austria in case Hitler moved his command there as the war neared its end. The 4th Armored Division then moved into Czechoslovakia to root out German resistance. When the war ended, Loring was in Volyne, Czechoslovakia, and remembered feeling "vast relief. It meant you had a chance to live. You could die almost any minute.

"You didn't have much to celebrate with," he said, "but what you had, you did."

With the war over, Loring's division moved into occupation duty in Landshut, Germany (north of Munich). He had made it through the war with some frostbite, but no other injuries. He had been promoted to private first class and received a number of honors, including the Bronze Star. And now, his college experience was about to provide some exciting opportunities.

"I'd had one semester of college, which put me in very exclusive territory, I'll tell you," he said. Loring was assigned to the Information & Education School, where he taught American soldiers who could not read or write. His job at the I&E School also gave him the opportunity to explore Germany and meet local citizens. He had studied German during his one semester at Bowdoin and was not fluent, but could speak enough to understand and be understood.

With the war over, Loring fell in love with Germany, a "wonderful place." Over the year he spent at the I&E School, he made many German friends with whom he stayed in contact for the rest of their lives. "You become friends with a German, you're friends for life," he said.

Because of his college education, Loring also had the opportunity to attend the Army's American University in Biarritz, France, where he studied American literature and German for two six-week sessions. He then decided to return to the I&E School in Germany to finish out his service.

As much as he loved Germany, he "was very anxious to get home. My family was waiting for me. My girlfriend was waiting for me. I wanted to get back to college and get going. I was twenty-three and thought I was an old man."

Loring graduated from Bowdoin College magna cum laude in 1948. After Bowdoin, "I wasn't ready to take a permanent position," he said. "I didn't really know what I wanted to do. I decided I ought to get married." On January 14, 1950, he married Marilyn Cummings, whom he had grown up with in Bath. Marilyn had been teaching school in Santa Cruz, California, so they moved there, but, after a bit, "I decided it was time to get serious."

The couple moved to Miami. After one night in a hotel, Marilyn walked into the Miami school office and was immediately hired. Loring enrolled at the University of Miami and got his master's degree in 1951. He then was accepted into Harvard University and they moved to Cambridge, Massachusetts.

As he was finishing his PhD in American literature at Harvard, Loring accepted a job teaching at the University of Kentucky. After one year at Kentucky, he decided that "the South wasn't for me." It was too hot and he needed to be closer to Harvard to finish his graduate thesis. He then accepted a job with the English Department at Norwich University in Vermont. He earned his PhD from Harvard and spent the next twenty-five years at Norwich, becoming a full professor, chair of the English Department, dean of the college, vice president, and then president of the school for ten years.

He returned to Maine in 1983 to lead the capital campaign at Bowdoin College, then was appointed interim president at Saint Joseph's College in Standish in 1987, and then president, holding that position until he retired in 1995.

Loring and Marilyn have returned to Germany several times since the war and have also visited Omaha Beach. He describes his military experience as a "million dollar experience that you wouldn't give a dime to repeat." By that, he means that his military experience earned him the G.I. Bill, which paid for his bachelor's, master's, PhD, gave him the money to buy his first home and continues to provide him medical benefits. His education gave him unique opportunities during his military service, and his service gave him the opportunity to spend the rest of his life in education.

18

GEORGE PACILLO

Never Back Down When You Know You're Right

During his service in the Army, fighting in the South Pacific, and, later, working for Central Maine Power, George Pacillo learned to never back down when he thought he was right.

Before the war, George lived on Deer Street, off Fore Street in Portland, near where Hub Furniture is. Deer Street was an Italian community. A picture of Benito Mussolini hung in the Pacillo home. George's father had emigrated from Italy in 1898 and had returned during World War I to fight for Italy. During World War II, with all three sons in the U.S. military, the FBI visited George's father and saw the picture of Mussolini on a wall. The FBI told him that he had to become a citizen and get rid of the Mussolini picture. He did both.

"They didn't want to send me to Italy because I could talk Italian," George said. "They figured if I got there, I'd never come back."

During the war, the State Theater in Portland used George's name and picture to sell war bonds.

In 1943, George was a nineteen-year-old Army private in the 129th Regimental Combat Team, based in the Fiji Islands. He was the youngest in his unit. "They used to call me Pooch because I used to hug the ground like a dog," he said. He had trained as a paratrooper and infantry member, learning "how to take a gun apart and put it together blindfolded." On Bougainville, in the Solomon Islands, he was about to see his first combat.

The Marines had established a beachhead where the Navy's Construction Battalion, or Seabees, needed to build an airstrip so fighters could land. "All we had was four miles of the island and the Japanese were on the end of the island," George said. "To get to us, they had to go through the most dense jungle in the Pacific. We set up pillboxes and tunnels going to every pillbox and a minefield out front. About 500 feet, we cleared it right out so we could see the enemy when they got here to attack us."

The jungle was so dense that the Americans had to cut through with a machete. George saw huge spiders with webs twenty-five feet in diameter, and giant centipedes and red ants. He also saw some animal five or six feet long that looked like an alligator that had been killed by the concussion of a mortar.

As they prepared for a Japanese attack, George and the 129th also had to repel constant night infiltrations from Japanese patrols. "Whenever you stop anywhere to take a nap, dig a slit trench," George said. "That way, you stay alive the next morning."

George went on patrol every week. "We got out there one time, about six miles out," he said. "We were out there with an officer from field artillery and we could hear chopping. We went down to investigate. The Japanese were building something." George called in artillery support. "We started getting shelled really close." But when he reported that the shells were too close, the artillery reported back: "We haven't fired any yet." The Japanese had spotted George's patrol, so they returned to their base and reported the Japanese location.

A few days later, in July 1944, some banana leaves were moving. A soldier shot at the leaves and the long-awaited Japanese attack began, right through a minefield. "We knew how to get out of the minefield and back into it without blowing ourselves up, but they didn't," George said. "They just came wave after wave. They're laying on the barbed wire. They're jumping on each other. It was really a turkey shoot." The Americans lost twelve men, but the Japanese "lost thousands."

George and the 129th then shipped to Luzon in the Philippines and walked all the way to Clark Airfield, the American airbase that the Japanese had captured. George earned the Bronze Star for his role in helping to retake the airfield.

On their way to Manila, General MacArthur ordered the 129th to wait so that the 1st Cavalry (which had been commanded by MacArthur's father during World War I) could lead the way into the city. There was a brewery near where they dug in. The company commander said: "'Dump the water out and help yourselves.' So we went over and shot holes in everything and beer was coming out of every tank in there. We filled all our water tanks with beer. We stayed there for four days and drank."

The 129th was then ordered to Baguio. As George's unit crossed the Passig River on rubber rafts, a Japanese company on the other side opened fire. George jumped into the river when they started firing but was shot in the leg. He made it back to shore and spent two weeks recovering. He received the Purple Heart and, later, received the Philippine Liberation Medal.

The 129th then followed the Japanese into the northern mountains, fighting them cave to cave until August 1945, when the war ended after the U.S. dropped atomic bombs on Hiroshima and Nagasaki.

With the war over, George did not have quite enough points to head home, so he was assigned to Japan. Despite the fierce fighting, he loved the Philippines and its people, learning some Filipino love songs that he can still sing today. "The people were very good to us, the Filipino people, but they took a heck of a beating," he said.

George landed in Yokohama, Japan, and spent three months in that country, even visiting Hiroshima. Everything was "scorched." Three months later, in November, George received his orders to go home. Before he boarded the *Intrepid*, his commanding general had one last piece of advice: "I don't want any one of you guys to raise your head to nobody but Jesus Christ." George understood that to mean to never back down if you think you're right.

"It's quite a journey I took," he said. "I'd never go and see these places if I hadn't been in the service."

When George finally arrived in Fort Devens in Massachusetts, just before Christmas, "they told me I had to wait a week before they processed my papers and everything, so I went over the fence and called a cab." George spent Christmas at his cousin's house in Worcester, Massachusetts, and called his parents. A couple days later, he was finally discharged and went home.

But he had malaria. As he got off the bus on the corner of High Street in Portland to greet his mother, he had an attack. "I was shaking," he said.

For five years after coming home, George was hospitalized every two to three months for malaria treatments. "When I first got it, I'd be sweating like hell and shaking," he said. "The doctors said the only way to get rid of it is, when it's cold and you don't want to go out, go out even though it's sweating. So I did what they said and I got headaches. I had all kinds of headaches. I said, 'oh the heck with it,' but, bang, it went away."

George has had good health all his life, except for the malaria. "I never needed any blood or anything. The way you see me is the way I came into this world," he said, pointing out that he does not have any missing or false teeth.

Even while recovering from malaria, George graduated from Northeastern University. His mother had saved all the war bonds he had bought during the war and gave them to him when he got married. He cashed those bonds in to build a home.

He also began working for Central Maine Power. "I did everything," he said. "You name it, I did it. I made electricity. I delivered electricity. I checked on electricity. I worked with linemen to make sure they did a good job. The last ten years, I was a line inspector. I didn't do anything!"

If he found mistakes, he would report them, even if it displeased someone. "When I disagreed with a boss, I don't care who it was, I disagreed with them because I knew it was right," he said, remembering his commanding general's advice. "And I never backed down when I knew I was right."

19

BILL LALIBERTE

Recognize and Preserve History

From appearing in a photo with "Ace of Aces" World War II fighter pilot Richard Bong to writing his own month-by-month memoirs, Bill Laliberte has always recognized the importance of preserving brushes with history.

On December 7, 1941, Bill was seventeen-years-old, driving home from church in his native Southbridge, Massachusetts, when the radio announced the Japanese attack. Bill, who was studying to be a machinist at the Cole Trade School and was working at the Russell Harrington Cutlery, spent the day listening to reports. By the end of the day, he had decided to enlist in the Army Air Force (at that time, the Air Force was part of the Army) to be a pilot.

Bill had made dozens of model airplanes as a kid, entering one model he built in a contest and winning a gas-powered model airplane. "I was very interested in aviation," he said. "I wanted to be a pilot." But the Air Force did not accept seventeen-year-olds, so he had to wait, enlisting the following March, right after his eighteenth birthday. After flunking his physical exam because of an inflamed left eardrum, Bill enlisted in the Regular Army.

With his dreams of becoming a pilot dashed, Bill returned to his passion for building model airplanes and enrolled in the Army's aircraft mechanics school in Biloxi, Mississippi. Later, he studied aircraft electrical at Chanute Field in Illinois. In March 1943, Bill graduated from Chanute Field and was stationed in Blythe, California, where he worked on B-17 aircraft, was promoted to corporal, and still found time to hitchhike to Hollywood to see Red Skelton perform.

In August 1943, Bill was assigned to the 305th Airdrome Squadron and promoted to sergeant. Six months later, in February 1944, his squadron shipped out of New Orleans on the USS *Sea Marlin*, a Victory Ship (bigger than the Liberty Ships). Bill was thrilled to travel through the Panama Canal. "When I was in high school, I had built a little model of the locks of the Panama Canal with gates that worked and everything," he said. "It was nice to see how it really worked."

The 305th Squadron's job was to manage airstrips and service aircraft. In April, his squadron landed at Aitape, New Guinea, a small village with half a dozen little thatched roof buildings and one building with a cross that they figured was a church. The infantry had invaded four days earlier and the Seabees (the Navy's Construction Battalion) had just finished building an airstrip. To build an airstrip in the Pacific theater, the Seabees would lay landing mats down on crushed coral. The landing mats were interlocking strips of steel, two feet wide and ten feet long with holes in them to make them lighter. The strips were interlocking so if they were bombed or otherwise damaged, they could be removed and replaced easily.

With major fighting still continuing, Bill's squadron immediately got to work, servicing American and Australian fighters and transport planes that could not make it back to their bases or carriers. As a sergeant, Bill was in charge of the airplane electrical department, despite being just nineteen years old.

One of his jobs was to run the landing lights, which were kept off unless an aircraft was arriving. "One night, I was out there, driving along the airstrip, checking things out, to see that the cords hadn't been cut or anything like that, and I saw what appeared to be a log in the middle of the runway," he said. "And I thought, what the heck is that log doing there? I came upon it and recognized that it was a snake, a python. I was in a jeep and I managed to drive the jeep over the thing and I parked the back wheel of the jeep on the thing and I remember him turning around and trying to bite the tire. I had my carbine but I didn't want to shoot because there might be Japanese somewhere around, so I took the hand crank of the jeep and smashed him over the head, put him on the front hood of the jeep and took him back to camp. As I recall, he was twenty-one feet long. If you're going to be afraid of snakes, that's one to be afraid of."

In October, Bill, who had been promoted to staff sergeant, and his squadron participated in the invasion of the Philippine Islands, landing at Tacloban on Leyte Island. Bill and the 305th spent their first night on the beach. During the night, the Japanese bombed the airstrip. "We had never heard bombs drop before and at first didn't realize what they were. In the movies, bombs always made a whistling sound. These made a whoosh-whoosh sound. When they landed on the strip about a hundred yards away, we knew what they were."

The Tacloban airstrip jutted a mile out into Tacloban Bay, facing a small hill across the bay. For several days after the 305th landed, Japanese fighters would fly around the hill and strafe the runway and the squadron's tents.

In early November, just before one such strafing run began, Bill had to go to the bathroom. Because no latrine had been dug, the "usual procedure was to go dig a hole, use it and fill it up." So he dug a hole about twenty-five yards from the mechanics' tent, "and was squatting over it when I heard machine gun fire. I looked up to see a Japanese Zero strafing the runway." The Zero was by him in an instant. Since he had not been hit, "I finished my mission."

Bill and his squadron were kept very busy at Tacloban, servicing the carrier-based aircraft engaged in the Battle of the Philippine Sea. They were so busy that, if a jeep was not available, Bill would ride a bicycle to the end of the runway to repair a plane so it could return to combat as quickly as possible.

While at Tacloban, Bill had what he recalls as a "brush with history," meeting Major Richard Bong, one of America's most successful fighter pilots during World War II, with forty aerial victories, 200 combat missions, and more than 500 combat hours. When General Douglas MacArthur presented the Medal of Honor to Bong at Tacloban, Bill and a buddy were standing in the background, in front of a P-38. The *Life* magazine photograph did not capture them, but Bill wrote about the ceremony years later for the History Channel's magazine.

After helping ready aircraft for the invasion of Okinawa, Bill and his squadron joined the invasion, arriving on Okinawa on the Fourth of July in 1945. Bill helped to prepare the B-29's for the bombing of Japan. While on Okinawa, Bill had another "brush with history," meeting General Jimmy Doolittle, the famous leader of the first bombing raid on Japan.

One month after he arrived on Okinawa, on August 6, 1945, the Americans dropped the atomic bomb on Hiroshima and, three days later, on Nagasaki, soon ending active combat operations. The war was not quite over for Bill, though, who was still working on planes at Okinawa. The next month, a typhoon devastated the area, destroying the kitchen and mess hall, and sending Bill and many others scrambling into the caves the Japanese had used during combat, in order to escape the storm. Luckily, everyone survived, and, in October, Bill was shipped to Japan. Two months later, he boarded the aircraft carrier *Lexington* to sail home. Ironically, the *Lexington* had been built to replace the original *Lexington*, sunk by the Japanese in 1942, which his father had helped build in the Fore River Shipyard in 1927.

Bill still had another typhoon and a bout with malaria to overcome, but, on January 13, 1946, he was discharged from the Army after three years, five months, and ten days of service.

"Somewhere along the line, I had lost the desire or ambition to become a pilot and I was no longer interested in working on airplanes," Bill said, so he enrolled at Franklin Technical Institute in Boston to study electrical maintenance and began working for an electrician under a program where the Veterans Administration paid 60 percent of his pay.

On November 13, 1948, Bill married Pauline Richard. Together, they raised four children: Ann, Billy, Jack and Patrice. In 1956, Bill went to work for J. J. Nissen Baking Company as an engineer at its plant in Worcester, Massachusetts. He moved to Portland in 1966 and became plant engineer. "There were zillions of machines and he kept them running," his daughter, Ann, told the

Portland Press Herald. "He would get calls in the middle of the night to go in and fix machines." Bill worked for the bakery until he retired in 1987.

Through the years, Bill has recognized his many brushes with history and, in fact, his direct involvement in the history of World War II, and has sought to preserve that history. In addition to writing for the History Channel, Bill helped write a history of the 305th Airdrome Squadron and has written a month-by-month memoir for his family. Bill also spent years leading tours of the Portland Observatory, serving as a Greater Portland Landmarks docent, and teaching countless visitors about Portland history.

Bill passed away on August 21, 2013.

20

ARTHUR O. CARON

The Most Important Missions Never End

Seventy years ago, a twenty-three year old Westbrook man set himself a mission to rescue his brother from the hell of a Japanese prisoner of war camp. Seven decades later, he is still trying to rescue that same brother from another hell just as personal and real.

Arthur Caron was born in Westbrook in July 1919, one of fifteen children; eight boys and seven girls. All eight boys would eventually serve in the American military, four during World War II. "There isn't another parent in the world that put eight boys into uniform," he said. But Arthur's desire to serve stemmed not only from love of country, but from a personal mission to rescue his brother, Albert, who was a Japanese prisoner of war.

In 1940, as his brother, Albert, enlisted in the Army, Arthur was twenty-one years old and working in the Dana Warp Mill in Westbrook. Arthur had served in the Civilian Conservation Corps and the National Guard, but had been discharged from the Guard when he married A. Elva Davis on June 15, 1940. When World War II broke out, Arthur and Elva had a young daughter, Judith.

Arthur also was an air raid warden for Westbrook, making sure residents pulled down their blackout shades at night so no enemy planes could target them. He covered Central, Brackett, Mechanic, Saco and West Pleasant streets.

But Arthur and his family had received terrible news. Albert had been captured by the Japanese Army at the fall of Corregidor in Manila Bay, on the Philippine Islands in 1942. Arthur had a new mission, to rescue his missing brother. "I thought it was my duty," he said. "Albert was my prime duty. I really wanted to go [to the South Pacific]. Probably wasn't a chance in a million I'd go there, but had to try."

So he tried to enlist in the Navy, but was rejected because he had a wife and young daughter. He tried again and was shocked to discover that his boss had obtained a deferment for him. "Who the hell are you to be getting deferments for me?" Arthur demanded, refusing the deferment. Two weeks later, he received his draft notice and was off to Plattsburg, New York, for training. He learned to disassemble and assemble .50 caliber machine guns blindfolded, and hoped he would serve in the South Pacific so he could look for Albert.

With that mission in mind, Arthur volunteered to go on a submarine or a PT boat (Patrol Torpedo boats used for fast attacks) in the Philippines, hoping to find his brother, or at least gather some news about him. "All I wanted to do was go to the Philippines," he said. But the Navy had other plans, assigning him to Naval Air Station Key West in Florida, where he was a crewman aboard a sub-hunting airplane. While serving in Florida, Arthur received a coconut with the inscription "10-6-44 NAS Key West," which he donated to the Westbrook Historical Society.

According to an interview Arthur gave in 2005, he briefly thought he had another opportunity to find Albert when he was ordered to ship out for China. He tossed his sea bag onto a truck and was walking up the gangplank when the Navy changed his assignment, ordering him instead to a prisoner-of-war compound in California.

Arthur was bitterly disappointed. "I thought I might find out something about my brother" during the assignment near China, he said in the interview, but he did his duty and reported to California, where he oversaw German prisoners of war until the end of the war.

He returned to Westbrook and was overjoyed to learn that Albert was alive and had escaped the Japanese. After fourteen months in captivity, Albert had escaped into the jungle. While the Japanese looked for him, "[h]e hugged a tree so hard that his imprint is still in the tree," Arthur said. Albert survived on wild pineapples, eating so many that they blistered the inside of his mouth, and led Filipino soldiers in raids against Japanese camps before making his way to Australia.

Back home, Arthur went to work at the S. D. Warren paper mill in Westbrook, where he worked for the next twenty-seven years. Arthur and Elva had three daughters before Elva passed away in 1983. Two years later, Arthur married Charlotte Wilson, who had two daughters.

"I'm one of the luckiest men in the world," he said, "because God gave me two good women. He gave me my first wife, which I had for forty-three years, and this second one for twenty-seven years. I'm trying to break that first record. She's very good to me.

"I'm no spring chicken. I'm an old turkey," he acknowledged, but "I must've done something right."

Arthur recently donated to the Westbrook Historical Society a scrapbook of newspaper clippings about Westbrook soldiers during World War II, including reports of his brother, Albert's, capture. And, even after all these years, Arthur is still trying to help Albert, who lives in Yarmouth and recently lost his wife after a battle with Alzheimer's. Albert went through "hell and high water" while captured by the Japanese, Arthur said, but, after losing his wife, "[h]is life is ending and he's still in hell." Arthur visits Albert as often as he can to sit with him and keep him company, finally fulfilling the mission he set for himself seventy years ago.

21

JIM MARDIN

Even If You Don't Have Much to Lose, You Still Have Much to Offer

Jim Mardin did not have much, growing up in South Portland, Gorham, and Portland, especially after his father left and his mother had to care for three children on her own, but he always had much to offer, starting with hard work.

Jim was born on January 23, 1922, in South Portland, the youngest of three and the only boy. He was five years old when his father left. Jim's older sisters, fifteen and seventeen at the time, went to work and Jim's mother paid a family in Gorham five dollars a week to take care of him. While he was in high school in Portland, Jim was back with his mother, sharing an apartment with her. She worked in the high school cafeteria and he worked at a grocery store after classes. Between classes and work, there was no time for sports or activities, and none for friends or girl-friends.

This was the Great Depression and times were very tough for many Americans, including Jim and his mother. But he pitched in and helped out, working every afternoon and each Saturday.

"I didn't have any friends in high school because I was working," he said, without complaint. "When I went into the service, it
was no different."

He enlisted in the National Guard in June 1940 at the age of
eighteen and was called up into the Army three months later. "I
think my generation was prepared when we went into service," he
said. "I had nothing to start with, so we had nothing to lose when
you went in there, and you learned as you were in the service."

Stationed at Fort Williams, Jim was trained on the 12-inch
guns protecting Portland harbor. He quickly achieved the rank of
Staff Sergeant, but felt like he had more to offer. "The war was
going by and I couldn't seem to be involved in it, just sitting in the
harbor, so I applied for engineer school." It meant reducing his
rank to private, but he accepted that so he could do his part in the
war effort. Unfortunately, Jim did not have a strong enough sci-
ence background and failed out of engineer school at Norwich
University in Vermont. Instead, he was assigned to an anti-aircraft
division in Camp Davis, North Carolina.

He became a clerk in the 460th Anti-Aircraft Battalion, part of
the 1st Army, 5th Corps. The 460th was equipped with 40 mm
anti-aircraft guns and .50-caliber guns mounted on a half-track to
protect artillery from planes. He sailed for England in January
1944 on the *Mauritania* as part of an advance party for his outfit.
On the way, the sergeant major got a bad back and Jim became
the new battalion sergeant major. Again, he had more to offer
than he at first expected.

Jim and the rest of the advance guard shipped out of South-
ampton, England, on June 9, 1944, and landed on Omaha Beach
on June 12, six days after the initial D-Day invasion. The rest of
the 460th arrived on Utah Beach on June 29. Because he was

based in headquarters and had access to a typewriter, he kept a log of where and when he moved, written either at the time of the events or shortly after. His entry for June 13 reads:

> France. Spent the early morning hours besides vehicles catching up on sleep. Many German planes flying around and the sky was red from the tracers.

After setting up the command tent in an apple orchard, Jim dug a foxhole for himself and covered it with timbers, then "[p]ulled guard with a rifle, whistle, and hand grenades." Wrote Jim: "Had a few raids and much firing was done although our CP area was never actually strafed. Germans at this time were in Cerisy la Foret, a large forest, just below us."

Although he was the top enlisted man in the 460th and worked in headquarters, he always looked for more ways to pitch in and help out, like pulling guard duty, checking out observation posts, or riding back with the messenger. "[I]n case anything happened, there were two of us," he said.

The 460th stayed in the St.-Lo area until the end of July, when the Allied forces finally broke out and began marching across France. During June and July, the sky was full of German bombs.

"I've never been so scared in my life as when the planes were strafing," Jim said. "That's your first indication that you're in war." His entry for July 28 reads:

> Left Balleroy, France for Cerisy-la-Foret, France. At this time, the breakthrough was being made. We arrived at the new area in an Apple Orchard late and had to dig in the CP tent. This area was covered with foxholes. Had no time to dig a foxhole of own and there were no foxholes in near vicinity. Just after dusk the action began. First we could see flares being dropped close

overhead but did not move until the scream of falling bombs could be heard. Dived for a truck. For the rest of the entire night the sky was filled with German planes making the trek back to the beaches or trying to blast the infantry out of their foxholes. Slept on top of the ground but was ready to dive for the truck if the flak began bursting overhead.

While growing up, Jim did not have much, which he credits with preparing him for some of the hardships of serving during World War II. While he occasionally slept in an old barn or an abandoned house, most of his time was spent sleeping in a tent, on the ground, or in a foxhole. During the summer and fall, it seemed to rain constantly. On August 18, Jim wrote that his battalion had camped for the night near Mortree, France: "CP tent was practically [inundated] by a rainpour one night. Same with pup tents. Miserable night all around.

"You're roughing it all the time," he said, recalling that soldiers would sometimes be transported behind the lines to take a shower and get powdered for lice. Jim recalls taking a shower in June 1944, soon after arriving in Normandy, but could not recall another shower during his service.

But all the soldiers, whether infantry, artillery, administration, or anyone else, did their part to help with the war despite the danger and the difficulties. "There were so many people there who did their job and kept the war going, protected the infantry," he said.

The 460th reached Paris at the end of August 1944, but "[w]e had to stay beside the road because the French Second Army went in first" to liberate Paris, he said. "We went in behind them with our equipment and the girls were throwing flowers." They then camped outside Paris in two-man tents and, once again, it was "raining buckets."

As the 460th moved into Belgium, and fall turned into winter, the rain turned into snow. Jim and his battalion never received the winter overshoes that they were supposed to get. By December 1944, Jim's feet had turned black from trench foot and he was sent to a field hospital.

"Nothing was going on," he said. "We were supposed to be safe."

But, in mid-December, the Germans began their counteroffensive, trying to drive the Allied Forces out of Belgium. This battle, called the Battle of the Bulge, became one of the most famous battles of World War II, and the field hospital where Jim was recovering was right in the line of attack.

"We were running ahead of [the Germans], trying to evacuate the patients," Jim said.

He wrote about the evacuations in a letter to his mother dated December 30, 1944. One Sunday morning, he woke to hear tanks and half-tracks on the nearby highway and gunfire. Someone reported that a German patrol "had us cut off," but Jim and the others thought it was "just another rumor." Then a bulldozer driver reported that he had come face to face with a Tiger tank. "He jumped off a bulldozer and came down to the hospital," Jim wrote. Shortly after, the hospital evacuated to a field hospital farther back from the front. "The field hospital was full and could not take us so we kept going further back which was just as well as the Germans soon took the town the field hospital was in."

The next evacuation hospital was full and sent them to another hospital, where Jim and the others got a few hours' sleep before a German air raid began. "I could hear the planes diving over us and our machine guns shooting at them," he wrote. "Then they started dropping bombs. The first ones were some distance from the hospitasl [sic] and only made a distant explosion. The last ones came closer and it scared h_ll [sic] out of me as I could hear the plane going low overhead and then hear the bombs whistle as they came down. One bomb hit quite close breaking the windows and shaking us up a bit. I expected to see the whole building come down on my head. Looking out the window I could see a building close by burning from a hit and also hear someone screaming."

Jim and the other patients were evacuated again. Altogether, Jim stopped at six hospitals in one day. "Trying to set a record," he wrote his mother.

After recovering, Jim was sent to a replacement depot to be assigned to another unit, but he wanted to return to his battalion. "I decided I wasn't going to stay there [in the replacement depot]," he said. "So early in the morning, about 6 o'clock in the morning, I got all the gear I had available and, it was all fenced in, but the guard helped me. He held the fence and I went under the fence." Jim then hitchhiked back to his battalion. When he reached his battalion, there was a letter waiting, stating that he had gone AWOL, but it was taken care of and he stayed with the 460th.

Belgium, with its pine trees and snow, was "[j]ust like being in Maine." As the U.S. Army prepared to cross the Rhine River into Germany, it captured the bridge at Remagen. The 460th defended the bridge for several days in February 1945, but the Nazis ultimately destroyed it, forcing the American troops to cross the Rhine on a pontoon bridge.

While in Germany, he saw his first jet fighter. "One day, I'm watching, and I see this German plane way up there," he said. "We'd watch the dog fights and could see the bombers limping home and the ground would be covered with bundles of foil. That's how they'd set the anti-aircraft guns off, by dropping that stuff. . . . All of a sudden, I saw four [American] P-38's take off. They're going to go up and get [the German plane]. They're going up and up and up. He's just sitting there, lazing along. All of a sudden, they got close enough, and he was just gone. That was the first jet. I didn't know what he was."

The 460th then moved into Czechoslovakia in May, as the war ended. Jim had so many points that he was one of the first soldiers to be sent back to England for transportation home. Soldiers needed to accumulate a certain number of points to be eligible to be shipped home after the war. The military awarded points for months served, being in combat, and other considerations. After a month waiting in England, he sailed back to New York. He was discharged at Fort Devens, Massachusetts, then took the train home to Portland.

Once home, Jim received fifty dollars a month from the government, but he also worked every job he could find: cleaning windows, shoveling snow off the railroad switches, digging potatoes, driving a pickup truck for a pickle factory, and painting buildings. Once again, even if he did not have much money, he still had much to offer: a drive to succeed, to work hard, and to get a good education.

He enrolled at Northeastern Business College in Portland to study accounting on the G.I. Bill. "You definitely need an education, as far as you can go," he said, stressing that the degree should be a practical one, like his accounting degree, to help land a job. After graduating, he became the office manager for a potato chip factory, where he worked for eleven years. Then he became the vice president of Merrill Transport Company for twenty-nine years.

Being a veteran, older than the other students at college, had some advantages, Jim said, like meeting his future wife. Bettie Bowen was nineteen and he was in his mid-twenties. "We were all veterans," he said, laughing. "It was pretty nice."

"She wanted a ride home," he said. And he had a car. He gave her a ride and they started going to dances and dating. They were married in 1950.

Jim and Bettie tried for years to have children, but could not. Instead of giving up, they found a way to make life work, and adopted their daughter, Tamlyn, in 1957, and their son, Timothy, the next year. Tamlyn has a daughter with whom Jim enjoys driving and Timothy has four children.

After their children were grown and Jim had retired, he and Bettie still believed that they had much to offer, and began volunteering at Maine Medical Center. Then Bettie suffered a stroke. After a year of intensive therapy, she seemed to be "doing fine," but developed Alzheimer's. Jim took care of her for a year at home until she fell. Then they had no choice and she moved into Sedgewood Commons, an Alzheimer's care unit in Falmouth. Jim visited her five days a week until she passed in May 2011.

Jim, now ninety, continues to volunteer at Maine Medical Center and was named the hospital's Volunteer of the Year in 2011. He has volunteered more than 9,000 hours for the hospital since 1988, most of them indexing records in the library's archives or distributing informational pamphlets in the oncology center. He also volunteers at Sedgewood Commons, where his wife lived.

And he volunteers at the Maine Military Museum and Learning Center in South Portland. Jim wrote a guide for all the items on display at the museum and an index to the brass plaques on the museum's walls, so family members can find a loved one. A lot of veterans come to the museum with their families. "It's good being here," he said.

Jim has always been willing to offer his hard work and his time. "I don't have much free time," he said, cheerfully. "I'm not a person who sits home and does nothing. I have to be doing something."

And, as he has done his entire life, he continues to offer perhaps the most valuable commodity of all: himself.

22

JOE BRUNI
Be a Family Man

For veterans like Joe Bruni, World War II was an important part of their lives, but it was what they did after returning home that defined them: earning a living and being a good husband and father. Many, like Joe, rarely talked about their service, not wanting to "brag." But, like Joe, they took the dedication and honor that they displayed during their service and brought it home with them, to be good "family men."

Joe was born in Portland on March 19, 1924; the youngest boy in a family of four boys and one girl. Instead of playing sports or activities at Portland High School, Joe shined shoes in his father's barbershop, "Eight Chairs, No Waiting," located first on Preble Street, then on Monument Square.

He grew up during the Great Depression, but was fortunate because his father's shop remained successful despite the tough economic times. "Growing up, I had it pretty easy," he said, "because my parents, my father, had his business and it was successful, so I grew up with the luxuries."

After graduating from Portland High School in 1942, he went to work at the Portland Company, a machine shop, making parts for elevators. "I didn't work there very long because my whole class was drafted," he said. "They drafted us very quickly."

"We all wanted to go," he said, recalling a friend sobbing outside the draft office because a heart murmur prevented him from serving.

One month after his nineteenth birthday, Joe took a train to Miami Beach for basic training; an eye-opener for someone who had never been out of Maine except to watch the Red Sox play at Fenway Park. "We got off the train at night and they wouldn't tell us where we were going, so it was a complete surprise," he said. "So we got off and we looked around and I saw palm trees and I said 'where the hell are we?' The sergeant said 'you're at Miami Beach.'"

Basic training at Miami Beach was quite an experience for a Maine boy who had grown up during the Depression, even one from a middle-class background like Joe. "We lived in the best hotels," he said. "I mean, going down and having breakfast, lunch and supper, we had silverware. We had plates. I mean, a lot of people don't believe this, but it's the God's honest truth."

After thirteen weeks in Miami, Joe was assigned to aircraft mechanic school in Goldsboro, North Carolina. He was a member of the U.S. Army Air Corps, the predecessor to the Air Force. Next came gunnery school in Greenville, South Carolina, then advanced aerial gunnery school in Fort Myers, Florida. While in Fort Myers, Joe was surprised to see female pilots and co-pilots on the training flights. They were members of the Women Airforce Service Pilots, or WASP's, and played a vital role in America's war effort, transporting planes and training crews. When he and his crew flew to Georgia to pick up their new B-25, he watched another B-25 land. "Beautiful landing," he said. "Hatch opens underneath. A WASP, a woman pilot, gets out. She was the only one on that plane. It was amazing. They were great."

With his new B-25, Joe and his crew flew across the country and spent a few days in Hawaii, refueling, before flying to the South Pacific. His first base was in New Guinea.

Joe was a top turret gunner on the B-25. His crew was a low-level attack outfit. Their principal job was to attack Japanese ships by flying just above the water, under the ship's radar. They would fly low over the ship, guns blazing, then fly away. Joe's B-25 had been outfitted for such assignments. Its nose had been closed off with seven .50-caliber guns placed in the nose. Two .50-caliber guns were on each side of the fuselage and Joe was on top. Because most of their missions were over water, they did not even have parachutes, but they did have an inflatable life raft.

Their goal was to fly below the ship's big guns, but it was harrowing. "Do you know how much lead was flying in the air?" Joe asked. Attacking ships was "[s]cary. I didn't care for that."

But they managed to stay under the Japanese ships' guns, just taking some light rifle fire. "We got hit a couple times, but nothing serious," he said.

Joe counted himself fortunate. "I never had very terrible experiences," he said. "I had scary experiences. I mean, anybody says that they weren't scared when they flew a mission, they're crazy. I mean, you never knew if you were going to come back or not. I lost friends overseas."

In addition to attacking Japanese ships, Joe and his crew also strafed factories on the Japanese mainland when they were based out of Okinawa and, one time, escorted a squadron of P-38's to

China. Joe's B-25 was left alone while the P-38's went on their strike. "If you don't think that was scary, being left alone," he said. "But, luckily, they came back and we flew back to the Philippines. That was kind of a scary mission."

Joe flew twenty-five missions in the South Pacific, based out of New Guinea, Palau, the Philippines, and Okinawa, and received the Air Medal. Once, he saved his crew's life, not with his gun, but by watching the instruments. They were flying out of Okinawa and it was Joe's job to watch the instruments during takeoff. When the pilot opened up the engines, the gauge for the left engine displayed "awfully, awfully hot." Joe insisted that the pilot stop the takeoff, telling him "I don't care to fly this." The pilot finally agreed and they taxied back to the hangar. When the crew chief inspected the engine, he discovered that the left engine had no oil because the supply was completely blocked by metal chips. The crew chief told the men: "You guys would've taken off, but you'd been airborne maybe a minute or two and that left engine would've cut off," Joe recalled. "We didn't have the altitude to do anything. [The crew chief] said 'you would've gone right in [the ocean].'" Joe had saved the lives of his crew.

Joe and his crew flew their last mission on August 4, two days before the United States dropped the atomic bomb on Hiroshima. The men did not know that America was preparing to drop such a weapon. "We never knew what was going on," he said.

The United States dropped a second atomic bomb on Nagasaki on August 9 and, six days later, Japan surrendered. Joe was watching *The Great John L* with other soldiers when "[a]ll of a sudden, someone screams in the back: 'the war's over!'" The soldiers jumped up, shouting and hugging each other. Then the skies lit up in celebration. "They opened up with everything on the island, on Okinawa, where we were," he said. "The sky was lit up. Tracers in the sky. Bombs exploding. They were shooting everything in the air. And guys were coming out of their tents *bang, bang, bang*. We all carried .45s."

With the war over, Joe and his crew returned to the Philippines, then sailed for San Francisco; leaving on Thanksgiving, but not arriving until December 10. He then boarded a train for a seven-day cross-country ride to Boston with no bunks and no showers. "How we must have smelled," he said.

By Christmas, Joe, who had reached the rank of technical sergeant, was discharged from the Army and was home. He was still only twenty-one years old. "You can imagine how young we were when we went in," he said.

He did not waste any time before returning to the Portland Company and getting on with the rest of his life. "The war was over," he said. "I was home."

He was dating a woman when she made the mistake of introducing him to her friend, Eleanor, or Ellie, Grant. "I took one look at her and that was it," he said. They dated for seven years before marrying in 1955. Joe and Ellie had six children in eight years: Sally, Kathy, Joe, Margaret, Elizabeth, and David. As they raised their children, Joe left the Portland Company and went into business with a cousin selling televisions, then worked for Nichols, a manufacturing company on Congress Street, until he retired in 1980. After retiring, he served at the bar at the Elks' Club, Sportsman's Bar and Grill, Sully's and then at the American Legion's Andrews Post on Deering Street in Portland.

Over the years, he rarely told his children or anyone else about his service in the South Pacific. "I don't tell them," he said. "What's done is done. I don't go around bragging." What has always been much more important to him is being a good "family man."

All of his siblings have passed away and, in 1998, so did Ellie. "She was a wonderful, beautiful lady," Joe said. "I loved her dearly. And I never wanted to be attached to anyone else. I had my family. That's all I ever wanted."

Joe's six children, seventeen grandchildren, and seven greatgrandchildren all live nearby. In fact, Joe lives with his youngest daughter, Elizabeth, in North Gorham. He loves having his family nearby and being involved in their lives. "I see a lot of them," he said. "We're very close."

"I love them," he said. "Anything they want, I give them."

When he sums up his life, he is proud of his service in World War II, but is careful not to "brag." Instead, he defines his life by the time spent with family. "I got married," he said. "Raised six kids. My wife passed away fourteen years ago and I live with one of my daughters and I'm very happy."

23

INEZ LOUISE (VARNEY) RONEY
Families Fight for Each Other

On February 13, 1943, the Marine Corps began recruiting women with the slogan: "Be a Marine . . . Free a Man to Fight!" Inez Louise Varney from Jonesboro, Maine, had an even more personal reason to enlist: She wanted to do whatever she could to win the war and bring her brother, a Marine, home as soon as possible.

Inez was born in Jonesboro, Maine, in Washington County on July 12, 1920. Her father was a school superintendent and state senator, and her mother took care of Inez and her two brothers. After graduating from Jonesboro High School, Inez went to Machias Normal School (a state teacher's school). Her first job after graduating from Normal School was teaching a combined first and second grade, for which she was paid $700 a year.

By 1943, women were serving in the WAVES ("Women Accepted for Volunteer Emergency Service," which later became the U.S. Naval Women's Reserve), the WAC's (the Women's Army Corps), the SPARS (the United States Coast Guard Women's Reserve), the Air Force's Women's Flying Training Detachment (WFTD) and the Women's Auxiliary Ferrying Squadron (WAFS), which would later merge into the WASP (Women Airforce Service Pilots). The Marines realized that they needed help filling a variety of noncombat jobs, and so joined the other Armed Services in welcoming women, setting a goal of 18,000 women recruits.

Inez was twenty-two years old and teaching in Winn, Maine, at the time. Her older brother, Richard, was already in the Marines. "And I thought if I could do anything to help bring him home, I would do it," she said. "And that's why I joined." She does not remember what her parents' reaction was to her decision. "I didn't tell them," she said. "I just did it."

To serve in the Women's Reserve, women had to "meet rather stringent qualifications which prescribed not only their age, education, and state of health, but their marital status as well," according to a history of the Women's Reserve written by Colonel Mary V. Stremlow, USMCR (Ret.). The women had to be United States citizens, could not be married to a Marine, could not have children under eighteen, could not be shorter than sixty inches and could not weigh less than ninety-five pounds. They also had to have "good vision and teeth."

After enlisting on April 17, 1943, Inez was sent to basic training at Camp Lejeune, North Carolina, then to Cherry Point, NC. According to Colonel Stremlow's online history, the women were given an aptitude test. The original intent for the Women's Reserve was to focus on clerical positions, but the scope of duties for the Women Reservists quickly expanded.

"More than half of all Women Reservists were engaged in clerical work—about the same percentage as in civilian life," wrote Colonel Stremlow. "But new ground was broken as women went to work as radio operators, photographers, parachute riggers, motor transport drivers, aerial gunnery instructors, cooks, bakers, Link trainer instructors, control tower operators, motion picture technicians, automotive mechanics, teletype operators, cryptographers, laundry managers, post exchange salespersons and managers, auditors, audio-visual librarians, assembly and repair mechanics, metalsmiths, weather observers, artists, aerial photographers, photograph analysts, chemists, postal clerks, musicians, statisticians, stewardesses, and writers."

On July 14, 1943, Inez entered active service as an instructor for pilots learning to fly in a simulator. "I had been a teacher and they needed teachers," she said.

"I had some interesting people that I worked with," she said, mentioning future U.S. Senator and astronaut John Glenn, future U.S. senator Joe McCarthy, and Brian Keith, an actor who starred in Disney's *The Parent Trap*, *The Russians Are Coming, The Russians Are Coming*, and is perhaps best known as "Uncle Bill" in *Family Affair*.

Inez then became a gunnery instructor, teaching Marines how to fire a machine gun.

She also kept in contact with her older brother, who received her letters even in the immediate aftermath of landing on Iwo Jima, and was "grateful" for her service. Inez's younger brother also enlisted in the Marines, but nearly died from undiscovered diabetes. A local newspaper published a letter from Inez to her younger brother, written as he prepared to leave for basic training, in which she sought to give him some advice on what his life would be like in the Marines and how to prepare himself for a life after the war. "It seems to be a Marine characteristic to be tough. You can be tough without being rough, don't forget that," she wrote. "I've seen so many people who have been influenced in the wrong direction since I've been in the service and most of them not more than twenty. There is seven years difference in our ages and I was all 'set' in my ways before I came into the service but you have a lot to learn and decide before you are quite settled, so use your good stubborn character, develop a strong mind and you will come back a good civilian ready to do what you want and knowing what you want. This isn't supposed to be a sermon. It's just that I want you to do the right things and have fun at the same time."

After the war ended and the Women's Reserve began to be disbanded, Inez returned to teaching. On June 28, 1947, she married Robert Roney, also from Jonesboro, who had been a sergeant in the Army during World War II. Together, they raised two children and have two granddaughters and five great-grandchildren. Inez taught for twenty-three years at several schools, including schools in Winn, Lincoln and Sanford, covering kindergarten through grade eight during her career. Inez even taught her daughter, Susan, kindergarten and first grade at East Sebago Elementary School, and two granddaughters third grade at the Baldwin Consolidated School. Robert died on November 10, 1997, and is buried in Sebago Town Cemetery.

Inez passed away on October 28, 2012, at the Maine Veterans' Home in Scarborough, Maine.

24

FERN GAUDREAU
Take Time to Think and Reminisce

After a busy life working in the South Portland shipyard, serving as a paratrooper in the 82nd Airborne, then delivering mail and driving a school bus while raising a family, Fern Gaudreau has come to realize the importance of taking time to think and reminisce about his life experiences.

Fern was born on November 12, 1921, in Westbrook, where he grew up with his four sisters and one brother, first on Myrtle Street, then on Bridge Street, then in a Westbrook Housing building on East Bridge. Fern's grandparents had moved from Canada to Maine to find work. His father worked at S. D. Warren in Westbrook while his mother took care of the home and family. He attended St. Hyacinth's Parochial School and, by 1941, was working at the shipyard in South Portland.

When the Japanese attacked on December 7, 1941, Fern was on his way to Lewiston to buy the "most beautiful Harley-Davidson motorcycle you ever saw." When he heard the special bulletin over his car radio, "I said to myself: there goes my bike." He still recalls the day with a wince of pain: "leather saddlebag, chrome . . . you wouldn't believe it. Five hundred dollars."

In 1942, Fern enlisted in the 82nd Airborne and shipped out to boot camp at Fort Bragg for infantry and jump training. Then he was off to England, to prepare to enter the war. In the spring of 1943, Fern was transferred with the 45th Infantry to invade Anzio, Italy. Fern also fought alongside the 42nd Regimental Combat Team through the Po Valley and Liri Valley campaigns in 1944, as the Allied Forces struggled to break through the Nazi and Italian resistance.

Fern did obtain a three-day pass while he was in Italy and visited Pompeii and Herculaneum. "Pompeii was destroyed by Vesuvius in 79 A.D. and Vesuvius was still smoking when we were there," he said. It was also in Pompeii that Fern saw, and fell in love with, his first opera. And he toured what had once been a Roman brothel, as a group of WAC's (Women's Army Corps) laughed at the paintings describing the services that had been provided.

In Herculaneum, Fern visited the catacombs, the tombs where bodies were hung on hooks instead of burying them. "I'm telling you, boy, there are some awful sights there," he said.

In 1944, Fern was transferred back to England to prepare for D-Day. He admitted that he was "scared stiff," preparing for D-Day. "There was a jumpmaster there, see. If you chickened out, he'd boot you out."

He vividly recalls the chaos of the airborne landings amid tracer fire, or the "little red balls coming at you."

"I landed a couple miles from my jump sight," he said. "It was dark. I remember coming to a farmhouse. Of course, I was able to speak French. This woman came out. It was a couple hours later. She said: 'American. American.' She couldn't believe her eyes."

Fern, and the other airborne infantry, had been scattered over miles and miles of heavily defended French countryside. The soldiers did not know where they had landed, or where the rest of their unit was.

"We began to consolidate, joined our unit," he said. One device they used was a small piece of bent metal, called a cricket. The soldiers were trained to "click" the cricket to identify each other in the dark. To this day, when Fern sees his barber, another airborne veteran, the two men say "click" to each other.

Once they found each other, the soldiers still had to overcome the tall French hedgerows, which often hid Nazi soldiers. "God they were thick," Fern said. "A tank couldn't go through." A soldier whom Fern knew, named Belanger, came up with the idea of welding a jagged piece of metal to the front of tanks, to help them cut through hedgerows.

After the soldiers finally broke through, Fern recalls waiting to enter Paris, to give General Charles de Gaulle and the French Army the chance to enter Paris first. But once he entered Paris, "wine flowed like water. People were hollering: Vive l'Amerique!"

Fern also fought in the Battle of the Bulge, in occupied Belgium. "We had to hold the flank," he said. "That was the 3rd Army's show. Boy do I remember the cold. And we did what we could. Everything that you could put on, you put on. We survived. Of course, we were much younger then. It was one of the coldest winters they had for years in Europe."

Once through Belgium, Fern crossed the Siegfield Line and invaded Germany. In one incident, Fern and his unit were taking sniper fire. They surrounded the sniper and were surprised to find that it was "a kid, maybe thirteen or fourteen years old. But," Fern recalled, "there was a German major with a P-38, a pistol. I wanted that pistol, so I grabbed it. He looked down at me and called me an 'American shwine.' I knew what that meant."

Fern's unit had two German immigrants: Herman Heller and Carl Dickler. Carl's family had immigrated to America recently, in the 1930s, and he had relatives in Heidelberg, so he asked the major if he could borrow a jeep to visit them. Carl went alone, but, when he returned, he told Fern what happened. "We parked in front of their building and they came out with their hands up, crying. And the women were crying. When they saw who it was, they could not believe their eyes. They had been told that when the Americans came in, they would rape all the women. Quite a reunion."

In another German town, Fern and Herman Heller saw German traitors hanging from all parts of the street. The two Americans needed a place to stay and knocked on a door where they saw candlelight in the window. A young, pregnant woman opened the door. "She looked at me and fainted," Fern said. "I said: 'Herman, she's going to have a baby.' So I picked her up in my arms and placed her on the sofa. Her father came home and Herman told him in German that we meant no harm. All we wanted was a place to sleep. We were given a nice bedroom, beautiful bed, and we could have had our throats slit. We slept there for a couple hours and when we got up in the morning, they had a nice breakfast for us. We didn't make out too bad."

Shortly after, Fern was wounded in Nuremberg and nearly lost his leg. "That's when the war ended for me," he said.

Having survived the horrors of combat, Fern almost died on the way to the hospital. It was midnight on "a beautiful moonlit night," he recalled. "All of a sudden, there was this plane coming and rattling of machine guns. I said 'What the hell's going on?' The bullets, you could feel them coming through the ambulance." A Luftwaffe fighter was strafing the ambulance despite its large red cross. "The other guys could get out, but I had to stay in." Fern held his breath as the fighter made two passes, but nobody was hurt. "Jesus, that was close."

He spent three months in a hospital in Nancy, France. While he was being prepared for surgery, the surgeon saw his name and began to speak to him in French. "I went through the surgery and a couple of days after the surgery, he came over to look at my chart and asked 'which French division do you belong to?' I told him that I was American, not French. We both got a laugh out of that."

In January 1945, Fern returned home on a cargo ship, calling it a "rough crossing."

"I remember in the hold, we were in the bottom of the ship, a lot of the servicemen were sick. Seasick. I was one of the few that wasn't sick," he said. "Jesus, after two, three days of that, I said I'm going to sleep up on deck. I don't care how cold it is." As he went up the stairs to the deck, he saw a childhood friend, who found him a place to sleep on the second deck, saving him from the seasick soldiers down below.

After the war, Fern sold tickets at the Prairie Mutual racetrack for three years, then worked at S. D. Warren, where his father had worked, for one year, before going to work for the U.S. Postal Service, where he worked for thirty-five years. Fern clerked for eight years, then walked a route for another nine years, before driving a truck to deliver mail in the Prides Corner area of Westbrook. Fern always enjoyed giving children rides in his postal truck. In 1952, Fern married Rita Briard and they had one son, who works for the Maine Turnpike Authority.

His war experiences "were something I took for granted," he said. "It's only as time goes on, you have to stop and think and reminisce. I haven't done this for years and years and years. You had to be there to really know the facts."

Once he took the time to reminisce, some of the darker moments of war came flooding back. As he and his unit were marching down a country road in France toward a small town, they came upon three young women, completely nude with their heads shaved, clutching pocketbooks. The women had fraternized with Nazis during the occupation. As punishment, the villagers had shaved and stripped them, and sent them out of town.

In another small town that had been shelled, Fern spotted a small girl hunched over some rubble. As he approached her, he saw an arm sticking out of the blocks of cement. The little girl was tapping the arm. "It was her mother's arm," Fern said. She'd been killed during the bombing.

But there were lighter moments, also, most involving food.

In France, after the Allies had captured Paris, Fern and his unit were patrolling the countryside when they saw a farmer stacking rounds of cheese in a field. "The cheese are like wheels," he said. "There must have been twenty, twenty-five in a mound." Fern never forgot what happened next. "He was covering them with cow manure," he said, laughing. "Come to find out, after they were all covered, probably four to five days or a week later, he would clean them up" and take a little bit off the top to market. Fern guessed that's why French cheese is so smelly.

Fern had another difficult experience with strange French cuisine on a date with a French woman. "She asked me if I wanted to have a good French dinner," he said. They went to a hotel and she ordered for the both of them. When the first course arrived, "they brought me a plate with a little bird on it. Now, the bird had been plucked, but the little legs were still on and the head was still on." He laughed. "I told her 'I can't eat that.' She understood."

But his strangest culinary experience may have been in Naples, Italy. "We were walking along and we had these two little old ladies behind us," he said. "They came up to us after a while. They didn't speak English, but they made themselves understood. They asked us if we wanted to eat a nice spaghetti and meatballs dinner. Well, after eating K-rations, C-rations, we went to their home, sat down, and had a nice spaghetti and meatballs dinner. It was really good."

But when he returned to his barracks and told the other soldiers about the meal, Fern began to wonder where the women had found the meat, since many Italians were starving and meat was extremely scarce. "One smart guy said 'You don't see any cats around here, do you?'"

After laughing for a long time, Fern admitted: "It was all right, but I wish I hadn't asked."

As important as it is to take the time to think and reminisce, with that story in mind, Fern suggested an even more important lesson to learn: "The next time you have spaghetti and meatballs, make sure it doesn't come from a cat."

25

DICK GOODIE

Share Your Stories

When Dick Goodie returned from World War II, he, like many soldiers, wanted to put the war behind him. That changed after his mother told him that "[a]nyone who has unusual experiences and doesn't share them with others by writing, is either lazy or selfish." Since then, Dick has written about and shared his experiences so that others could learn from them.

Dick was born on March 27, 1923, in Bangor, Maine, the middle child, with three younger brothers and two older sisters. His father was a portrait photographer, but when the Great Depression hit, the Goodie family found itself homeless, and moved to Bucksport, Maine, where Dick's father worked at Maine Seaboard Paper Company, fixing the conveyors that transported logs from the yard to the grinder. His father also played violin and had a dance band called "Goodie's Moonlight Orchestra," in which Rudy Vallee played before he became famous.

Dick was also musical, playing trumpet in the high school band. "I didn't do good in high school," Dick said. "I was a C student. I was more interested in hunting, fishing, and baseball."

After graduating, Dick went to work at the Bucksport paper mill on a paper machine.

On December 7, 1941, Dick was at his parents' home when their neighbors heard the news that Japan had attacked Pearl Harbor. "I couldn't make any plans for the future after that," he said. "I knew I'd be drafted."

Rather than waiting to be drafted, Dick tried to enlist in the Air Force to become a fighter pilot, but was rejected because of poor eyesight. Shortly after, he received his draft notice from the Army. In January 1943, Dick said goodbye to his family and girlfriend and boarded a train from Bangor, to Fort Devens, Massachusetts, for basic training. Three weeks later, Dick shipped out to Camp Davis, North Carolina, where he was assigned to the 486th Antiaircraft Battalion.

At Camp Davis, Dick learned how to use and operate an armor-plated half-track, .50-caliber machine guns, and 37 mm automatic cannons. Dick also returned to his musical roots, playing reveille each morning and taps each evening.

The training was rigorous. "We had to crawl through the mud under barbed wire with machine gun bullets going over our heads," he said. To prepare the soldiers in case they had to fight in the Pacific, a colonel made them camp in the swamps for three days. "We cut down trees and made rafts to sleep on," he said.

There were no alligators in the swamps, but there were snakes, a fact that panicked Dick's group one night.

"We're all formed in a half circle, the whole battery," Dick said. "They had these salamanders that looked like small alligators. They were green. North Carolina's famous for salamanders. When we first got to North Carolina, our captain said 'You have to be careful of the coral snakes. You have fifteen minutes to live [if you're bitten]. You have to get immediate attention.' We're all bug-eyed, sitting on our helmets in a circle. Suddenly, a salamander crawled between a guy's legs and the group panicked. The captain jumped off the trailer . . . [and] his driver was up a tree."

But Dick worked hard and was named squad leader by the time he turned twenty. He also acted as the referee during mock war maneuvers in Louisiana, to see which squad reached high ground first. He narrowly missed being paralyzed during one of these maneuvers.

"One night, we left at three o'clock [in the morning] to try to get the high ground," Dick said. "I was on top of a machine gun. Machine guns in those days were water-cooled and heavy. This guy was driving without lights. He went off a bridge sideways and I fell in a stream. The fifty caliber machine gun fell on my legs. It's a wonder they didn't break. I was on crutches for five weeks. They called me gimpy after that because of the way I walked. Quite a few guys got killed during the maneuvers."

After completing the maneuvers in Louisiana, Dick and the 486th in early December 1943 boarded the *Queen Mary*, an ocean liner that had been converted into a troop transport ship. The *Queen Mary* had made so many journeys through the German U-boat-infested Atlantic that Hitler had offered an award of one million reichmarks and an Iron Cross to the U-boat captain who could sink the famous ship.

Dick crossed the Atlantic Ocean safely and reached Glasgow, Scotland, where they had the chance to relax before continuing on to England for more training. "We went to Glasgow one evening for a dance," Dick recalled. "They had a 'rubber floor' with some kind of springs that would give a little lift. Before we went in, Ironfield [another squad leader] and I went in and this pretty girl would frisk us for bottles of whiskey. They didn't want any soldiers to enter with any bottles or flasks. Well, Ironfield went out the back door and came in again to be frisked by this pretty girl again. . . . In the Army, there are plenty of characters."

In England, there was much less time for socializing. "We ran every morning for five miles with combat boots that must've weighed five pounds," Dick said. In addition to regular training, Dick worked to become proficient with the anti-aircraft guns, firing at targets towed behind planes.

While in England, Dick and the men lived in Nissen huts, prefabricated metal buildings in the shape of a half-circle. Every night, from when he arrived in December 1943 until late May 1944 when he moved into the quarantine pens prior to D-Day, Dick heard B-17's returning from bombing runs over Germany.

"Some were really shot up," he said. "[O]ne guy came into the Nissen hut and said there's a B-17 just over the trees with two engines gone. One night, a soldier said a plane glided in with one engine. We all ran out. Sure enough. Three engines were feathered, just one engine was going. I can still see that airplane. They must have jettisoned everything. It was shot up pretty bad, but it limped in."

As the time to invade Normandy neared, Dick and the other men were sequestered in exit pens so that they would not inadvertently let any important information slip which could jeopardize the invasion. Dick and his men landed on Omaha Beach on June 23, 1944, under heavy shelling from the Germans.

"The First Division was five or six miles inland. They were anxious for tanks to help hold the pastures that they had won," he said. "After we took the waterproofing off our vehicles, we got on line that afternoon. Oh man, then we were really into it. I can still see the skies that night. Two huge armies, going in different directions. That was our baptism of fire. The artillery was terrible. Dead cows were around. Dead German corpses were around."

It was a quick and brutal introduction to war. On that first night of combat, Dick met a soldier from the 1st Infantry Division. Part of the man's arm had been ripped open by a bullet. Dick tried to convince him to return to an aid station, but the man wanted to stay with his unit. As Dick ducked back into his foxhole to escape the German artillery, he was amazed by the man's dedication to his fellow soldiers. "He taught me a lot," he said.

In Normandy, Dick helped the Allied forces break through the German lines at St.-Lo. "We helped on the breakout of the tanks," he said. "Two thousand bombers came over from England. To this day, I can still feel the ground tremble. They carpet-bombed the area around St.-Lo five miles wide and three miles deep."

After St.-Lo, Dick fought at Avranches and then in the Falaise Pocket, where the Allies destroyed the German Seventh and Fifth Panzer Armies. The battle, centered around the small town of Falaise in Normandy, was one of the decisive engagements and opened up the path to Paris and to Germany.

The battle was brutal. The Allied forces had surrounded the German Army and turned the meadows around Falaise into killing fields for the escaping Germans. There were literally fields of dead German soldiers. "I sat on a dead German's chest and ate my K-rations," Dick said. "There wasn't any place to sit. That's how conditioned we were as soldiers. . . . It was so brutal at times. On the other hand it was necessary to acclimate yourself to battle" in order to survive.

Near Falaise, Dick's squad was briefly surrounded by the enemy. "We got surrounded for about a day and a half there," he said.
"We got on the radio for air support. It was such a pleasure to
watch the P-47 Thunderbolts dive. I was mesmerized by that
airplane—a seven-ton, single-engine fighter with four-bladed
propellers eight feet across. They came in so low that day that
their clips from the machine guns would fall on our helmets.
Eight guns blazing. The Germans called them Jabos. How many
Germans surrendered because of those attacks? There's no accu-
rate count. That plane did a great deal to win the war."

After the Falaise Pocket, Dick and the Third Armored Division sped across France towards Paris, but were held outside the
city so General de Gaulle could lead his French troops into Paris.
"We could see the Eiffel Tower as we went around Paris," he said.
"We got to Paris about 10 or 10:30 [in the morning]. There were
still Germans in Paris at that time. They held us in reserve. Fifteen thousand soldiers. One of the heaviest divisions. The Second
and Third Armored had fifteen thousand. They held us in reserve
from 10:30 in the morning until two in the afternoon because
they wanted the Second French Division to go in and allow de
Gaulle to march [into Paris] first as a symbol of freedom."

Dick then headed east to Soissons, on the Aisne River. As he
and his men stopped near the town, Dick heard voices coming
from a nearby cabbage patch. Dick and another soldier captured
the German soldiers hiding in the patch. Because his squad had
to keep moving and could not take prisoners with them, "we tied
the prisoners to a tree so the American soldiers behind them
could take them back to a POW camp."

After fighting through France, Dick and the 486th Antiaircraft
Battalion entered Belgium, where they saw and heard of the hor-

ror of life under the occupation of the *Schutzstaffel*, or SS, the elite Nazi paramilitary unit. Locals told him and his men how the SS would machine-gun children who watched them march by, just to send a message that resistance would be met with fierce retaliation.

While in Belgium, Dick and his squad were moving down a road when he saw a little boy crying on the side of the road. He stopped his half-track and got out to talk to the boy, who told him that the SS had just shot his parents in their home nearby. Dick and his squad investigated and found them dead in their kitchen. Enraged at the murder of defenseless civilians, Dick and his men went looking for the SS.

They found the SS troops camped at a coal mine down the road from the boy's house. Dick's squad quickly set up their machine gun, but a bushy tree was blocking the gun's sight and the high-explosive shells that the gun had would explode in the tree. So, risking being spotted by the SS, who greatly outnumbered his squad, Dick crawled across the pasture to the tree with a saw and slowly cut it down and lowered it to the ground. Then Dick and his men opened fire on the SS soldiers. As the Germans retreated into the coal mine, Dick and his men raced across the field with nothing but hand grenades and threw them into the mine shaft, killing the rest of the SS.

After Belgium, Dick and his unit captured the first German city, Rotegen, and participated in the siege of Aachen. The city of Aachen was part of the Siegfried Line, a string of forts, anti-tank devices and other defensives measures designed to stop invaders. The Allies wanted to breach the Siegfried Line at Aachen and then move into Germany's industrial base, the Ruhr Basin. The 486th was stationed outside of the city and had to shoot down

German planes to protect the American infantry fighting in the streets and the artillery, which was providing cover for the infantry.

The siege was long and difficult, and "miserably wet." It had rained long and hard during the fall of 1944, which caused the ground to turn to mud. Dick's half-track sank into the mud and became unmovable. After a month of fighting, the Allied forces finally conquered Aachen, but both sides lost thousands of soldiers.

One of the things Dick learned during combat was the importance of keeping a sense of humor despite the brutality. It was the only way to keep sane and get through the war. During the siege of Aachen, a squad member Dick nicknamed "the Optimist" because of his upbeat personality walked into their makeshift shack, tossing a grenade back and forth. This, obviously, made the squad nervous. Then the Optimist pulled the pin out of the grenade and said: "Look. These things are perfectly safe so long as you hold the handle down." As the squad shouted at him to put the pin back in, the Optimist started coughing and dropped the grenade.

The squad had ten seconds to get out of the shack before the grenade exploded. In their hurry, the men knocked over the shack, then dove into their slit trenches, shallow excavations big enough for one man to lie in, and waited for the explosion. Instead, all they heard was the Optimist laughing. He had removed the gun powder from the grenade, making it useless. Dick and the rest of the squad broke into tears laughing at the trick.

We "had a genius of humor among us," Dick said.

After surviving the siege of Aachen, the 486th was assigned to stabilize the lines in the Battle of the Bulge in occupied Belgium, as inexperienced American forces had been forced to retreat. The ride from Germany to Belgium was dangerous on the rough, icy roads, and trucks frequently collided. Dick's mission was to secure a hamlet held by soldiers from the 1st Division. On the road to the hamlet, German mortar rounds and shrapnel clanged off his half-track, but his squad survived uninjured and arrived at the hamlet, where a major in a jeep stopped Dick and told him to set up behind a church. As the major and Dick were talking, a mortar round exploded near them. A piece of shrapnel from the mortar went through the major's helmet, killing him instantly.

Inside the church, the Belgian villagers had gathered, with their dead laid out in the center aisle. Back outside, Dick spotted a shed that he thought could serve as a place to set up camp and to get out of the cold winter nights. He decided to check it out. Just as he reached it, the shed blew up in his face. "Someone must have had their sights on me," he said.

Instead, he spent the entire night of Christmas Eve wide awake and prepared for a German counterattack. Thankfully, the counterattack never arrived. Instead, Dick and his men enjoyed some chocolate cake and coffee on Christmas morning.

Once the Battle of the Bulge was finished, the 486th had one last campaign: to invade the heart of Germany. Their target was the Ruhr Basin, the industrial center of the German war effort, referred to as the "Pittsburgh of Germany."

"Our job was to encircle the Ruhr Valley," he said. Unfortunately, Dick's force did not meet up with the other forces because four German Tiger tanks stood in their way. "We used to tremble even when we saw their tracks," he said.

The four Tigers knocked out the first seven American Sherman tanks. Three Shermans got through the ambush with some infantry, but "one of those Tigers came out of the woods and ran over half-tracks and trucks, like they were papier-mache floats in a holiday parade."

Finally, an infantryman knocked out the Tiger with a bazooka and Dick and his men set up at a crossroads and waited. When an artillery officer suggested that Dick's squad pull back because their light-armored half-track was no match for the Tigers, Dick and his men decided to hold their ground and support the infantry and artillery as best they could.

"We started cutting brush to cover the sharp lines of the half-track," he said. "The battle was still raging below and it started to become dusk. An officer from below wandered up from the woods, disoriented, saying 'I lost them all. I lost them all.'" Dick sat the officer down and gave him some water, but the officer soon left, continuing to mutter about losing all of his men. The Allied forces ultimately won that battle, but Dick never forgot that each victory had painful costs, like the officer losing all his men.

In addition to the devastation of battle, Dick also witnessed the horrors of Nazi barbarity when he helped liberate the concentration camp at Nordhausen. The Nazis had used slave labor from Nordhausen to build laboratories and testing sites for the V-1 and V-2 rockets. "Hitler made displaced persons, inferior races, as he thought it, work seven days a week, eighteen hours a day, digging through parts of the Harz Mountains," Dick said. By the time the American forces liberated Nordhausen, the inmates were barely even recognizable as human beings. They could not make eye contact with the soldiers and acted like "abused animals." One of the reasons Dick continues to talk and write about his war experiences is to convey his disgust at the Nazis' treatment of those they considered "racially inferior."

Once the war ended, Dick's unit was assigned to guard a women's de-Nazification camp near Stuttgart, Germany. The camp's goal was to de-Nazify 800 women of varying European nationalities who had worked for the Gestapo and the SS in jobs such as telephone operator or secretary. These re-education camps were part of a larger Allied effort to remove Nazi leaders from German society and to eradicate Nazi philosophy or symbols from German life.

While guarding the camp, Dick earned the last few points necessary to be sent home. He immediately went to work at First National Warehouse on Reed Street in Portland, typing progress reports and serving as the night watchman. He also enrolled at Portland Junior College. Because he had not done well academically in high school, Dick took a "cram course on algebra, English, writing, and so forth."

While at Portland Junior College, he discovered a love of writing, composing comical sketches for assemblies. He even wrote a play for the Drama Club, which was broadcast on the radio. He then transferred to Denver University and studied writing. After graduating, he worked for a while in California, then returned to Portland, Maine, to work for the railroad, where he stayed until he retired.

Dick and his wife, Joyce, loved exploring Maine with their girls, Laurie and Liz: hiking, cross-country skiing, downhill skiing, and fly-fishing. After all of those early-morning runs in basic training, Dick fell in love with distance running. He was one of the early organizers of road races in Maine, directing or co-directing five annual Maine Masters-sponsored races in the late 1960's and 1970's. Dick was inducted into the Maine Running Hall of Fame in 1992.

Writing about his experiences has also been a life-long passion for Dick. After his mother's admonition not to be selfish, but to write about his war experiences, Dick knew that she was right. Before beginning to write, he spent his first winter home, reading a stack of books about previous wars next to the furnace in his parents' cellar. After that, he began to write and write and write.

Over the years, he has published a tremendous number of essays and short stories. In 1961, he sold his first piece to the *Enterprise*, a weekly published in Lisbon Falls. In 1979, he received the Maine Press Association's Best Sports Feature for an article in the *Portland Press Herald*. In 1984, he published *The Maine Quality of Running*, a history of long-distance running in Maine. In 1997, he published *A Bracelet for Lily*, a love story set during World War II in occupied Belgium, which is available on Amazon's Kindle. And in 2010, he published *Raindrops on a Nail Keg*, a collection of essays about his life.

For Dick, writing, particularly about World War II, is a way to connect the past to the future and to make sure that others can learn from what happened.

As he wrote in *Raindrops on a Nail Keg*:

"Those of us who survived the war, no longer possessing the raw power of youth as when we soldiered, but mellowed to the gentle recollection of our army, still wonder if contributions made then, in some small measure, can help stabilize the capricious world in which we live today.

"If this can be true, then it will be possible to look back to those exciting days of the campaigns with renewed belief that they were indeed, the best years of our lives."

Dick currently lives with his wife Joyce in Westbrook, Maine.